Dame of Sark

The Dame of Sark

SIBYL HATHAWAY

Dame of Sark

AN AUTOBIOGRAPHY

First published 1961

ACKNOWLEDGEMENTS

Grateful acknowledgement is made to Mr. Robert Graves and Messrs. Cassell for permission to quote from *Goodbye to All That* by Robert Graves.

CONTENTS

LIST OF ILLUSTRATIONS

FOREWORD

I regret so much that my great-grandmothers
never kept diaries — the paternal one about life
in Guernsey during the Napoleonic Wars, and
the maternal one about life in Montreal during
the 1812 war against the United States — that
I am going to try to remedy that loss by writing
this account of seventy-odd years of life for my
grandchildren, hoping that they may have the
keen interest in the past that I always had, encouraged by my father. It is to him that I owe
my character and my real interests in life. He
taught me to be self-reliant and to think for myself, and I must never let it be forgotten how
much I owe to him even when I must tell tales
of my life with him.

Sark, 1960.

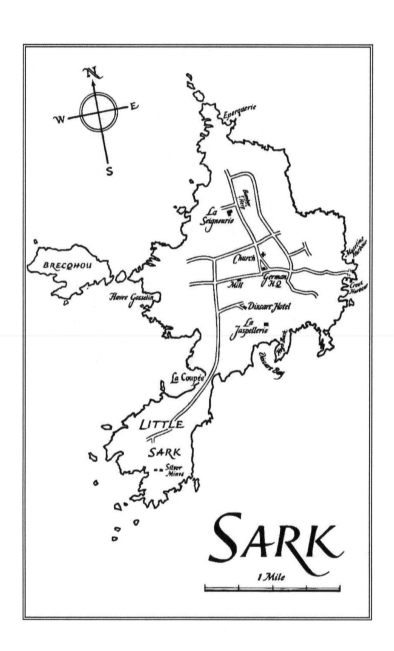

N

W   E

S

Eperquerie

La
Seigneurie

BRECQHOU

Havre Gosselin

Church

Mill

German
H.Q.

Maseline
Harbour

Creux
Harbour

Dixcart Hotel

La
Jaspellerie

Dixcart Bay

La Coupée

LITTLE

SARK

Silver
Mines

SARK

1 Mile

CHAPTER 1

THE ISLAND STORY

I was a month old when I first came to Sark, carried ashore from a small, storm-tossed sailing boat in the arms of an old fisherman on a day so wild that the weekly Guernsey Packet could not put into our tiny harbour. At the time of my birth there was no resident doctor on Sark, so I had been born at Hirzel House, a family place in Guernsey which once belonged to my great-great-grandfather, John Allaire, privateer.

Jersey, Guernsey, Alderney, Sark, Herm and Jethou form a group of islands which we call the Channel Islands and the French call 'Les Iles Normandes'. These islands are the oldest possessions of the British Crown, and the last territory remaining to England of the old Duchy of Normandy. They lie across the rock-strewn Gulf of St. Malo off the coast of Normandy and Brittany. Owing to the concentration of the tidal wave in this bay, it has dangerous races and there have been many wrecks in these waters.

More than a thousand years ago (in 933 to be exact) the Channel Islands were made over to Normandy, that turbulent province of France which had a series of prodigious rulers — such men as Rollo the Gigantic, William of the Long Sword, Richard the Fearless, Robert the Devil, and William the Conqueror. It must have been a happy moment for the King of France when William crossed the Channel although, as a result of his coronation as King of England, his native Normandy together with the Channel Islands were lost to France.

Later, England lost all her land in France but she kept the Channel Islands, and the Islanders have remained loyal to the English sovereigns as representatives of their own Norman dukes.

Sark (we call it by its ancient name of Sercq) is the only one of the islands which continues to be a purely feudal tenure and I, as the Dame of Sark, owe my allegiance to Queen Elizabeth II as my over-lord.

My father, William Frederick Collings, was the twentieth Seigneur of Sark. He never had a son, and as the elder of his two daughters I was destined to become the feudal chief and owner of the last bastion of feudalism in the world.

Sark is the highest and the most enchanting of the Channel Islands. There is a strange contrast between its wild coastline of high rugged cliffs dropping sharply to the sea, and the peaceful fields and moorlands which these granite cliffs support three hundred and fifty feet above the waves. The centre of the island provides wonderful grazing fields for our soft-eyed Guernsey cattle, and there are many wooded valleys which, in the spring-time, are so thick with primroses and wild hyacinths that the ground is flooded with a pale golden light or is as blue as the sky above. The rocky ground sloping down to the harbour is covered by a wild-flowered patchwork of sea-pinks, ragged robin, mauve aubretia, sea campion fragile and white as a sea-spray, tufted saxifrage, sheets of bluebells and clusters of wild pansies, which the country people call 'heart's ease'. Along the coast, the rocky precipices are fringed with ferns, heather and ivy. On every peak and headland great patches of gorse blaze brilliant yellow against the skyline. From early spring to late autumn, Sark's gardens are vivid with colour.

Every part of the coastline has a character of its own. The Gouliot caves are only accessible at low tide, and their walls glow with millions of rainbow-coloured sea-anemones interspersed with almost transparent zoophytes, each of which holds a drop of water so that the whole effect is iridescent. In some bays it is possible to find semi-precious stones such as agate, cornelian, and clear pieces of crystal, like amethyst or topaz.

The island is three and a half miles long and one and a half miles wide, and it is divided into three parts. On the west of Sark is

Brecqhou, a small sliver of land parted from the mainland by a narrow strip of sea and a nine-knot tide. Great Sark is joined to Little Sark by a unique causeway called the Coupée, thirteen feet wide and three hundred yards long. This raised road runs two hundred and forty feet above the sandy beaches and sea below. Before any carriage drives over it, the passenger must get out and walk on foot.

In former days only the sloping beach at Le Creux and the artificially hewn tunnel gave access to the island, and there was an occasion when the Lords of the Admiralty, wishing to land and inspect the defences of Sark before the harbour was built, sailed round and round the island, vainly seeking a landing place and finally sailed away declaring it was inaccessible.

Lying within sight of Normandy, with a population still speaking a dialect originating within that province, it is not surprising that the Channel Islands maintain many of the ancient Norman customs in spite of the fact that for nearly nine hundred years the islanders have been subjects of the British Crown. By far the oldest of the feudal customs which still exist in the Channel Islands is the 'Clameur de Haro'. In ancient days if a person was assaulted or any trespass committed on his property he thrice shouted the word 'Haro' and anyone who heard it was bound to come to his assistance. If the wrongdoer escaped, the cry was repeated from district to district throughout the whole Duchy of Normandy until the criminal was apprehended. In this way the system made every citizen a constable and escape was almost impossible. Nowadays the injured person, after having repeated the Lord's Prayer, cries aloud, 'Haro, Haro, Haro. *A l'aide, mon Prince. On me fait tort.*' This matter is then deferred for the decision of the Court and no further action can be taken until the plea has been heard. During recent history the 'Clameur' has been almost entirely confined to disputes over property and it has been raised only twice in Sark during my lifetime.

The *patois* differs in pronunciation in each island but it is still fundamentally old Norman French. Both my sister and I were brought up to speak this as well as modern French. In Sark the *patois* has survived in its original purity through a period of more than four hundred years; for the Sarkees are well educated and speak in addition good French while their English is often purer than that of many of the visitors.

An important part of Sark's history dates back to 1563 when Sir Helier de Carteret, Seigneur of St. Ouen in Jersey, journeyed to London and petitioned Queen Elizabeth to grant him the island so 'that it may be protected, cultivated, and be no longer a repair of pirates'.

Two years later, on 6 August 1565, he received a charter from the Queen under the Great Seal of England, granting it to him, his successors or assigns in perpetuity, for the sum of the twentieth part of a Knight's fee, now valued at fifty shillings, paid annually at Michaelmas. To seal this grant Queen Elizabeth sent a present to Sir Helier of *'six belles pièces d'artillerie'* from the Tower of London. One of these, made of bronze, with the inscription 'Don de Sa Majesté la Royne Elizabeth au Seigneur de Sercq. A.D. 1572' still visible, remains to this day on the Battery behind the Seigneurie, together with trophies of several wars.

The charter stipulated that the Seigneur must keep 'forty men at least, Our Subjects . . . each armed with a musket' for the defence of the island. Thus it became necessary for the first Seigneur to bring forty families — all but two were from Jersey — and allot to each a plot of land or tenement on which to settle. These properties were to descend from father to son or, failing a son, to the eldest daughter. Descendants of those forty colonists still live in Sark today and hold their tenements by the original tenure. Even today tenements cannot be divided, left by will, or mortgaged, or sold without the *congé* of the Seigneur, who can buy it himself or refuse a sale if the purchaser is not approved by him. If the sale is approved he takes the 'treizième' or thirteenth share of the purchase price. Land reverts to the Seigneur if the owner should die without an heir in the sixth degree of affinity, though only one property has fallen to the Seigneur for lack of an heir in my lifetime, and that to my father.

De Carteret set up a scheme of government partly manorial (or feudal) and partly parochial, which still holds good. Although the island is included in the bailiwick or district of Guernsey, it has a Court of Justice of its own whose officers are appointed under the recommendation of the Seigneur or his female equivalent who is known as 'La Dame'. There is also a Court of Chief Pleas, our Parliament, many of whose members are descended from the original owners of the forty tenements. Divorce is forbidden. Income tax and death duties are non-existent. The Seigneur himself can sell the island and all its rights, but only by consent of the reigning sovereign.

As well as the 'treizième' and land rights there still remain some curious ancient customs. For instance, the tenants pay a feudal due in capons on their kitchen chimneys. All grain milled for profit must be ground at the Seigneurie. There is a fine for either shooting a gull or taking gulls' eggs because the cries of the adult bird are a valuable indication of rocks ahead during the sea mists in winter.

For another good reason pigeons may not be bred by anyone except the owner of the Seigneurie. This is because they are inclined to eat the seeds of corn and the islanders like to husband all their resources. Every now and then carrier pigeons are blown off course and land on Sark. Technically they should have their necks wrung if they do not fly off home when they have recovered from the buffeting which brought them ashore, but everyone is too kind-hearted to carry out the letter of the law.

The Seigneur has the 'droit de Colombier' or pigeon-cote, and in my pigeon-cote all the pigeons are white. It is also laid down that only the Seigneur is allowed to keep a bitch. This law has been strictly enforced by the Chief Pleas since 1689.

The island's officials include the Seneschal or Judge, the Greffier or Clerk of the Court and the Prévôt or Sheriff. These three with the representatives of the forty families plus twelve selected deputies constitute the Chief Pleas or Parliament. This assembles three times a year in the presence of the Seigneur or his legally appointed proxy and has the power of making new laws and regulations for the island

and fixing necessary taxation, provided such enactments meet with the approval and consent of the Seigneur, who holds a limited right to veto. The Seigneur cannot sit in his own Court as judge, but has the right to appoint a Sénéschal who is sworn in by the Guernsey Court and before whom all cases are tried. In certain cases, appeal to the Court of Guernsey is allowed.

None of the privileges which were granted to Sir Helier de Carteret by Queen Elizabeth I has ever been annulled, though some of them have fallen into abeyance. Nevertheless they are still capable of enforcement at any time.

The de Carterets were Seigneurs of Sark from 1565 to 1720. Then the island was sold to one James Milner, who sold it to his son-in-law, the Bishop of Gloucester. He in his turn sold it in 1730 to Madam Susan le Pelley. The le Pelleys were Seigneurs of Sark during the Napoleonic campaigns when my great-great-grandfather, John Allaire, was engaged in the highly profitable business of privateering. He was one of Guernsey's many privateers who made a large fortune out of this practice.

There was, of course, a distinction between privateers and pirates. The privateer armed and commanded a vessel of his own: he held 'Letters of Marque' granted officially by the State to the captain of the vessel and he entered into a formal agreement with the crew. For example, after they had captured a ship and her cargo was sold, the money was divided into stipulated shares. One fifth went to the King and the remainder went to the owner of the vessel, officers and crew, according to seniority. Some of these Letters and Agreements are printed in full in the article on 'Guernsey Privateers and Smugglers' contributed by Mr. Lindwood Pitts to the *Guernsey Sun* in 1892. Privateers were supposed to run up the flag of their country when capturing an enemy vessel, but many of them had no hesitation in flying other colours when it suited their purpose.

One of my ancestors, Thomas du Bois of Guernsey, held a Letter of Marque which read as follows:

'Anne, by the Grace of God etc. etc.

'Whereas our said Commissioners for executing the office of our High Admiral aforesaid have thought Thomas du Bois fitly qualified who hath equipped, furnished and victualled a ship called the *Hope*, privateer, of the burthen of about eighty tons, whereof the said Thomas du Bois is Commander. . . . Know ye therefore, that we do by these presents grant Commission to, and do license and authorize the said Thomas du Bois to set forth in warlike manner the said ship called the *Hope*, privateer, and by his own command and with force of arms to apprehend, seize and take the ships, vessels and goods belonging to France and other our enemies their vessels and subjects or others inhabiting within any of their countries, territories or dominions, etc. etc. . . .

'Provided always that the said Thomas du Bois keep an exact journal of his providings, and therein particularly take notice of all Prizes which shall be taken by him. . . .

'And we pray and desire all Kings, Princes, Potentates, Estates and Republics, being our friends and allies, to give the said Thomas du Bois all aid, assistance and succour in their ports with his said ship.

'Given at London, 4th day of May, 1711.'

Pirates were unauthorized robbers on the High Seas — they held no commission or delegated authority from any sovereign or State. As often as not the crew consisted of seafaring men from many countries who signed on in a ship where no questions were asked and no wages paid, but every member of the crew took a share of the profits which might accrue from the voyage. One of the formalities of a newly formed pirate crew was the drawing up and signing of the Ship's Articles, taken from those of Captain John Phillips of the *Revenge*, which were written out and sworn on a hatchet for want of a Bible. The articles included such rules as:

1. Every man shall obey Civil Command. The Captain shall have one full share and a half in all prizes; the master carpenter, boatswain and gunner shall have one share and a quarter.

2. If any man shall offer to run away or keep any secret from the Company he shall be marooned, with one bottle of powder, one bottle of water, one small arm, and shot.

3. If any man shall steal anything in the Company, or game to the value of a piece of eight, he shall be marooned or shot.

4. That man that shall strike another whilst these articles are in force shall receive Moses' Law (that is forty stripes lacking one) on the bare back.

5. That man that shall snap his arms or smoke tobacco in the hold without a cover to his pipe, or carry a candle lighted, without a lanthorn, shall suffer the same punishment as in the former article.

6. If any man shall lose a joint in time of an engagement, he shall have four hundred pieces of eight; if a limb, eight hundred.

7. If at any time you meet with a prudent woman, that man that offers to meddle with her without her consent shall suffer present death.

Whereas the privateer flew under the colours of various countries, the pirate chose the most frightening flag with which to intimidate the ships he attacked, usually black, with a skull and crossbones or skeleton.

A common source of piracy was the privateer who drifted into bad ways in a ship that sailed under a Letter of Marque, which fact was pointed out by Cotton Mather, the New England divine, who said in one of his hanging sermons: 'Privateering stocks easily degenerate into the piratical, and the privateering trade is usually carried on with an unchristian temper and proves an inlet into so much debauchery and iniquity.'

It seems likely that john Allaire was a renegade privateer. Though a Channel Islander, he had the reputation of running up a French flag when he decided to capture an English ship. Circumstances favoured his nefarious exploits. In those days, French and not English was the common language in the Channel Islands, England was at war with France, and Napoleon was making every effort to secure control of the Channel. So, when the privateer's ship flying a French flag and manned by a French-speaking crew sank an English ship, the English assumed, quite naturally, that they had been attacked by the enemy. It would have been unwise to land the booty on the coast of Guernsey: the island was much too large and reports would soon have reached England. But the smaller grim Jethou, which Allaire owned in the early eighteen hundreds, was ideal for the purpose. The rocks round about are a death-trap for those who have never sailed in that part before and the treacherous tides can only be negotiated by the natives. The house which he owned there, is supposed to be haunted. Doorless and with its windows yawning, it stands to this day in a derelict garden, and one of his guns is still to be seen on the island. Apart from Jethou, which was used as his headquarters for privateering, John Allaire had two properties in Guernsey, one of which was later used as the Government House, and was also haunted.

There seems little doubt that John Allaire was guilty of an unchristian temper, debauchery and iniquity and, truth to tell, it seems likely that the fortune he gained by his exploits enabled his daughter, Mary, to become the Dame of Sark. She was his heiress and she married my great-grandfather, Thomas Guerin Collings of Guernsey, where the family lived. It was not until she was an old woman that the le Pelley of the day lost his fortune in a grandiose scheme for working silver and copper mines on the island. When the mines failed and his capital was exhausted, he moved his family away and obtained what money he could by leasing his personal property on Sark. Eventually he sold the island to my great-grandmother, Madame Mary Collings, and from then on my family was required by

Charter from Queen Victoria to uphold all the ancient laws and customs.

Since Madame Collings was a widow she became Dame of Sark. Being too old to take any part in the administration of the island, she delegated power of attorney to her son, the Reverend William Thomas Collings, my grandfather.

Grandfather Collings fell in love with the island at first sight and no one could have inherited a fief with more enthusiasm than he did. When he took over, Sark was suffering great poverty. The former Seigneur had spent absolutely nothing on the island; people who had gone to work in the mines had lost their jobs; the small resources of the island were no longer sufficient for the needs of the population; the oyster fishery had ceased and the other fisheries were not very productive; the Seigneurie had lost its old prestige; the grey-walled gardens had been left uncared for and many of the island's houses were deserted.

The Seigneurie had been moved by the Le Pelleys from the original manoir to the site of St. Magloire monastery. Part of this house had been in existence in 1565. My grandfather added a wing and because it was important to be able to signal to Guernsey nine miles away across the sea in an emergency, such as an S.O.S. for a doctor, he built a tower of local granite on top of the house. The ancient tower below could no longer be used for signaling because the trees had grown too tall, so rather than cut down the trees Grandfather built his hideous Victorian excrescence. He bought another farm at the back of the Seigneurie to extend his property down to the sea, and built new roads round the boundaries to make the house more secluded. He was full of fantasy, plunging a window through one of the rocks that tower over the Port du Moulin and making a cathedral-like window in the garden wall. This still adds to the difficulty of growing things in that part of the garden, as the wind whistles through the window.

Few gates on the property escaped one of his elaborate arches. It was not long before all these improvements attracted visitors to the island and excursion steamers began to arrive two or three times a week from Jersey and Guernsey. The gardens and grounds of the Seigneurie, now opened to the public, soon regained their old prestige. Larger hotels were opened, houses were put in order for letting and money began to flow into the island. Although farming and fishing are the main industries, Sark depends on the tourist trade for its prosperity. The money my grandfather invested in the island paid the islanders big dividends. Small wonder that they valued their new Seigneur.

My grandfather had at one time been Canon of Wells Cathedral and as an ordained man he naturally took a great interest in the church. He was responsible for building on the chancel and replacing the high pews with lower ones which made it almost impossible for the congregation to doze off during the interminable sermons of his day. People talked then of 'going to the sermon' and one of the roads leading to the church is still called La Rue du Sermon.

Sark's militia also came under his watchful eye. The ordinances from the year of his succession until two years before he died were regularly punctuated with orders for the improvement of its equipment and discipline. The forty able-bodied men with musket and ammunition furnished by each Seigneur under the charter of Queen Elizabeth had become the basis of the Royal Sark Militia, and Grandfather as hereditary Commandant (promoted to Lieutenant-Colonel by the War Office) must have cut a dashing figure as a fighting ecclesiastic at the head of his army of farmers and fishermen. My father was at one time Grandfather's Adjutant, but he never came to the command of our army. The Sark Militia, though gallant in aspect, faded away without battle honours. It had been non-existent for almost half a century when it was finally struck off the Army List in 1900.

Grandfather died before I was born, but, judging by his portrait which hangs in the dining-room, he must have been remarkably good-looking. There is something poetic about his face and the expression of his fine hazel eyes. It is easy to imagine that many of the young ladies of Guernsey might have lost their hearts to him, and as the family came from Guernsey it was only natural that he should marry a girl from that island. I'm told that he had been in love with a certain Mary Ann Lukis but was forced to marry her elder sister Louisa, who could not be left unmarried. Neither of them was beautiful, in fact they were both downright plain, but Louisa was perhaps the better of the two not only in looks but in intelligence.

Sark attracted much attention during my grandfather's time and in 1855 there appeared in a magazine edited by Charles Dickens a strange account of a visit to the island, in which the writer made an amusing reference to Grandfather: 'The present Seigneur is a refined and courteous gentleman, who has only lately become possessed of the Seigneurie, and his surprise at his own powers is greater than that of his subjects who have a firm belief that he is the equal in power and dignity of Queen Victoria. All that the Crown lays claim to in England in the way of mines and treasure trove and royalties are, in Sark, the Seigneur's. Half profits from wrecks are also paid to him, from which he derives no mean income.'

Although the climate of Sark is perfect from early spring to late summer, during the winter months the island is usually shrouded by mist or lashed by heavy storms which made it impossible for the boats to arrive from Guernsey or for the fishermen to put out to sea more than once or twice a week. So the families who could get away to Guernsey usually spent the winter there. My grandfather and grandmother were no exception. During their absence the Reverend Monsieur Cachemaille, the Chaplain, acted as Deputy Seigneur. He kept a daily journal which he sent over as a sort of serial by any boat that happened to be sailing to Guernsey. On one occasion he ended by noting, 'I am told that the Seigneurie is on fire. I go to see——' As the boat took an indeterminate number of hours crossing the stormy sea before it reached St. Peter's Port my unhappy grandfather could do no more, when the letter reached him, than get out his telescope and gaze anxiously across the water for signs of smoke. It would have been interesting to know what he had to say to his chaplain later about the false alarm. The erudite Monsieur Cachemaille came originally from Geneva and helped my grandfather to decipher a journal from which all our knowledge of the early days on the island comes. This ancient book was compiled during the colonization of Sark from Jersey in 1565, at a time when the people of Sark could only speak French, and was written by Eli Brevint, a minister of the Reformed Church, in a mixture of Latin and French. It was found in the rafters of the old Seigneurie when the house was being re-thatched. Presumably it had been hidden there when an invasion from France threatened the safety of the island.

From the day he set foot on it until his death, Monsieur Cachemaille never left the island. His nerve had been shaken by seeing a former Seigneur drowned when his boat capsized in a squall. Even as a very old man the Chaplain preached highly dramatic sermons about St. John in the island of Patmos, to whom he attributed the same dread of the sea. It was he too who wrote an account of Grandfather's influence on the island at the time he took over, in the course of which he noted that hitherto no member of the royal family had ever put foot on Sark. But as several personages near the Queen had visited the island and described its beauty to her, it seemed likely that Her Majesty would visit Sark in passing through the Channel.

Hopes of the visit ran high when the Admiralty sent the royal yacht *Osborne* to look for a safe anchorage at a convenient place, but lamentable weather intervened; rough seas indicated all too clearly that it would be both difficult and uncomfortable for the Queen to land and the great expectations came to nothing.

However, when she visited Jersey in 1859 she passed close to Sark and coasted all along the east side. The islanders supposed that she intended to disembark, but no. Her ship continued to steam away *en route* to Jersey. My grandfather ordered a salute to be fired in her honour, which no doubt she heard distinctly. All this time, still hoping for a visit, the whole family was down at the harbour. The old arched rocky tunnel leading up from the harbour was decorated with flowers, flags were flying, my grandfather was at the head of his militia in full regalia, standing on the red carpet which had been laid down on the temporary landing-stage, and a banquet worthy to be set before a queen had been spread out in the dining-room of the Seigneurie. But meanwhile an unforeseen disaster occurred. Peacocks had entered the dining-room through the french windows and ravaged the table. They scattered the flower decorations with their many-eyed tails (which are supposed to bring bad luck), broke irreplaceable glasses and plates, then strutted screeching among the havoc they had wrought. It was just as well that the Queen did not land.

Most of what survived the peacocks' raid was lost later when my grandparents were shipwrecked off the nearby island of Herm, while making their annual remove from Sark to spend the winter in the family house in Guernsey. As usual a steamer had been chartered for the occasion and although this 28 November 1872 was a very stormy day, the whole family and servants with cases of silver and valuables of all kinds had embarked in the tug *Gosforth*. At about five o'clock, when it was already nearly dark, the captain missed seeing the post marking a reef between Herm and Jethou. The ship struck and began to sink rapidly. There was only a small boat, into which scrambled ten persons in all. After rowing in the teeth of the tide for two hours, during which they were almost swamped several times, the women having to take off their petticoats to sop up the water and wring them over the side, they at last reached Herm. The pet dogs swam off the ship but were drowned, and although the family released their parrot it never reached shore. Everything on the ship was lost, including the original charter given to Sir Helier de Carteret, a copy of which was, however, safely in the Records Office in London.

Unfortunately my father was extremely insubordinate, madly obstinate, fiercely self-opinionated and prone to outbursts of uncontrolled rage. Worse still, he was violently anti-clerical and showed very little interest in improving the island which would one day be his. Yet, in spite of his faults, he was a generous man and a wonderful companion when he was with those he liked. Temperamentally he and his father were incapable of getting on well together. It was left to my grandmother to keep the peace between them, but with the best will in the world this was an impossible task. Grandfather wanted my father to go into the Church and he wanted to go into the Army. But permission was not given and Father flatly refused to go to his father's College — Trinity, Cambridge. Fearful rows ensued and in the end Grandfather compromised with a Grand Tour which took my father in a round-about way to Copenhagen.

My grandparents accompanied Father as far as Paris. On arrival, which was shortly after the débâcle of Napoleon III, Grandfather acquired a set of Regency chairs said to be looted from the Tuileries. This must have been his only recorded lapse from rigid morality, and it is rather a comfort to know that he was capable of human failing. In the family portraits which hang in the dining-room my grandparents and parents are seated on these chairs and today I have them in use not only in the dining-room but also in the drawing-room and sitting-rooms.

By an extraordinary coincidence, during Father's stay in Copenhagen a case of family silver and books was washed up on the coast of Jutland. Because my grandfather's name and address were still legible in the books, he received a letter from the British Consul which enabled Father to go and identify the case as being part of the luggage lost by his parents nearly two years before off Herm.

Father finally returned to Guernsey with no profession and no income. After his return he apparently lost his heart to Lily Langtry, whom he met in Jersey and who was then Lily Le Breton, daughter of the Dean of Jersey. (I found a treasured photograph of this very lovely girl after my father's death among his private papers.) A couple of years later he met and fell in love with my mother, Sophie Moffatt. She was born in Montreal of three generations of Scots Canadians, but as she never kept a diary or a letter and seldom talked of herself we have no record of her life in Canada except a sketch of her home, Weardale Lodge in Montreal, and a photograph of her at a fancy dress ball given there in honour of a visit from Prince Arthur, afterwards Duke of Connaught. The photograph shows a gay scene on ice in an elaborately decorated tent, everyone on skates. It was on a visit to London from Canada with her mother that she had developed pleurisy and been recommended the climate of Guernsey as ideal for her convalescence. There she encountered my father, William Collings, who was like no one else in the world.

He had no means of supporting a wife but was so determined to marry her that he swallowed his pride and agreed to carry out his father's wish that he should go into the Church. By this time he was in his late twenties and too old for Cambridge, so he reluctantly went to Durham and took his B.D. But Fate had other plans, which was just as well because he had no vocation and would never have been a credit to the Church. His father died just before he was to be ordained and he returned to be Seigneur of Sark.

The following year he was free to fulfil his wish and marry.

Although she was not strictly beautiful my mother was charming to look at, tall and graceful, with prematurely grey hair and fine hazel eyes set in rather a long face. Fortunately too she was blessed with a delightful sense of humour, self-discipline and a good temper. My father led her a life of constant worry and uncertainty, but in spite of it all she remained devoted to him. It seemed to me that she had the disposition of a saint.

Father was a fine-looking man, more than six foot tall, solidly built, with wavy black hair and intensely blue eyes which would blaze into an almost insane fury when he had taken too much drink. He might be normal for months and then suddenly the urge to drink would seize him. There was nothing unusual about the wines served with meals. In those days most men were accustomed at dinner to drink sherry with their soup, hock with their fish, Burgundy with their meat, claret with their game, and port to round off the meal. It was the quantity of liqueurs and brandy drunk afterwards that seemed to do the damage. Too much drink inflamed his temper to such an extent that he would shake his fist at anyone who had the temerity to disagree with him. When in the throes of his fury he could be really alarming.

Father lacked Grandfather's genuine interest in his inheritance and did nothing to improve his property. Mother was a home-loving woman and did her best to keep up the appearance of the Seigneurie, which deteriorated with the years because Father refused to spend a penny on it. He would say of the house as he said of any one of his frayed-cuff suits, 'It will last me out.' And Mother did not argue with him for fear of getting embroiled in a fearful scene.

My privateering great-great-grandfather, John Allaire

Myself in 1889

CHAPTER 2

UNCONVENTIONAL GIRLHOOD

It must have been a shock for my parents to discover when I was three months old that one of my legs was two and a half inches shorter than the other. As a tiny baby I was so swaddled in long petticoats, flannel wrappers and shawls that no one noticed the uneven length of my legs until I was 'short-coated'. At this time my mother found out that my nurse, Lizzie, suffered from epileptic fits, and it was assumed that she had dropped me during one of her seizures. She was hastily transferred from the nursery to the kitchen as cook, but by that time the damage was done and I was fated to be lame for life. One of my most terrifying childhood memories is of Lizzie lying rigid in a churnful of cream which she had upset on the dairy floor. In my mind's eye I can still see her dripping cream and being carried upstairs by John Hamon, the cowman. She was replaced by my much loved Nana, who watched over me in the nursery until I was old enough to graduate to the schoolroom, which was presided over by a governess, while my baby sister Doris occupied the nursery with Nana.

I may have inherited my bad temper from my father or my childish tantrums may have been caused by my lameness. On one occasion I clouted the housemaid with her dustpan because she did not get out of my way on the stairs. Needless to say, I was severely punished and my father carried me upstairs raging and struggling and shut me in my room. I was in such a fury that I threw the water jug, basin and soap dish out of the window. There was a skylight below, over the pantry, and I can remember enjoying a feeling of revenge when I heard the crash they made falling through the glass on to the stone floor below. 'That's what they get,' I thought, 'for shutting me away from my dog and my donkey.'

When I was four years old Mother took me to see a specialist in London. The trip was a great adventure. It took twelve hours by sea from Guernsey to Southampton and then there was all the excitement of travelling by the first train I had ever seen. Even now there are people in Sark who have never seen one. There are no railways in the Islands, and the inhabitants seldom take holidays in England or on the Continent.

Mother and I stayed in London with Mother's Canadian father, George Moffatt. He lived in a tall Victorian house in Westbourne Terrace near Paddington Station, and I was taken by my mother's old American maid to see the trains puffing in and clanging out of the station. One day we were rewarded for our vigil by seeing Queen Victoria arrive from Windsor.

For me the visit to London was spoiled by the clothes I had to wear. I particularly detested a black and white checked pelisse and bonnet garnished with a white ostrich feather and tied under my chin. The specialist who examined me offered to operate in an attempt to correct the dislocation in my right hip, but Father would not hear of it, so I was made to wear a surgical boot. No punishment could have been worse for me than that monstrous boot. It had a thick sole and heel which always felt wobbly, and because I was accustomed to the shortness of that leg, which never really impeded me, I felt hampered rather than helped. To add to the physical inconvenience, I was made miserable by other children who stared with avid curiosity whenever they caught sight of me. I cried so much that my mother came to the conclusion I would be better off without the boot and it was discarded.

Although the trip to London had been exciting, it was wonderful to get home to Father and Nana. Father always treated me more like a son than a daughter. The toys that normally appeal to small girls had no attraction for me. I disliked dolls and by the time I could appreciate my rocking-horse I was already mounted on a live one. Father filled the nursery and schoolroom with books which I enjoyed wholeheartedly. Between the ages of nine and ten I read *Masterman*

Ready, Midshipman Easy, The Last of the Mohicans, and Rolfe Bold-
erwood's *Robbery Under Arms,* and had started on Henty. I despised
the goody-goody books for girls that my aunts gave me. We had, and
have, our own fairy-tales and ghost stories on the island, which were
as familiar to me as the Seigneurie and no more frightening than my
own nursery. I knew that the ledges below the chimneys of all old
houses in Sark — including the Seigneurie — were for the witches
to rest on instead of coming down the chimney and putting spells
on the house and its people and animals. It was well known that the
evil eye could cause cows to cease giving milk and infest with fleas or
lice those people who were opposed to the possessor of 'the eye'. In
fact, any unforeseen domestic calamity could be attributed to this.

Tchico, or Old Dog, was supposed to belong to a witch and roam
the roads, even crossing the Coupée at night, but is never seen now
— though I was told that he once came to announce a death. This
legend of a black dog is not rare and I was interested to read in *A
Ghost Hunter's Game Book* by my friend James Wentworth Day that
'the legend of the Black Dog is common throughout East Anglia. It
is supposed to be derived from the Norse myth of the Hounds of
Odin, and to have been brought here by the Vikings'.

We know that the Channel Islands were occupied by the Vikings
— the progenitors of the Dukes of Normandy — so what can our
Tchico be but another ghostly Hound of Odin?

Fairy pipes, *'pipes de fétiaux',* were sometimes unearthed while
digging foundations or ploughing. They are tiny clay pipes with miniature barrels, probably the first pipes made when Sir Walter Raleigh
was Governor of Jersey and introduced tobacco as a rare and costly
luxury. The islanders were convinced that they had belonged to the
pouquelayes — the 'little people' — who they thought inhabited the
dolmens and menhirs, burial sites and votive stones dating from the
earliest known occupation of the island. The pouquelayes could be
very helpful if you put fresh milk out for them to drink and would
make the cream ripen so that the butter came quickly (though some
farmers' wives had more faith in throwing a coin into the churn —

always a silver florin because of the cross on it). They would also finish your knitting for you, and find things if you lost them. But if you made them angry by not believing in them or doing any mean trick, they would get blackberry bushes to scratch you or make you add up wrong or stop the hens laying. The most important thing to remember in dealing with the pouquelayes was to take neither count nor tally — *'n' en prendre ni compte ni taille'*.

Even today some old man will claim that he has seen fairies, and when laughed at by the young will retort, 'It does not mean that because you have not seen any, it cannot happen now.'

One of the legends of Sark concerns a certain well. It is said that anyone bold enough to draw water on Christmas Eve is sure to hear a voice calling him by name and will die before the year is out. This superstition was once put to the test many years ago when a bold man decided to prove whether it was true or false. He became so elated by the thought of his bravery that he drank too much brandy before midnight and when the moment came to test the superstition he fell into the well and was drowned. This certainly proved the story as far as he was concerned, though he was unable to leave any record as to whether he had heard the voice or not.

There is also a legend about the Eve of St. John. It is believed that at midnight all the cattle can be found on their knees and at that moment are gifted with the power of human speech.

My great-uncle Frank Lukis of Guernsey, a well-known archaeologist, taught me always to keep a sharp lookout for any flint arrowheads or stone implements whenever I walked across ploughed land. Our present Infants' School stands on the site of an early mediaeval cemetery. When it was being built a quantity of old stone roofing tiles were found as well as some skeletons in stone graves. Oddly enough the skeletons' heads were laid to the east and rested on stones. These stones now form the base of the railing enclosing the school yard.

A.D. 565 marked the arrival in Sark of the Welsh Saint, Magloire, with sixty-two followers from France. Saint Maglorius (from the Gaelic MacGlor — Son of Glory) and his disciples built their monastery on the spot where the Seigneurie now stands, above a boisterous brook. They made three ponds for carp, a dam and a water-mill for grinding their corn.

According to the *cartulaire* kept by the monks the monastic routine of Saint Maglorius was constantly being interrupted by raiding pirates. These were often Scots, and one Edward Bruce is several times mentioned. Before the year 1100 a high outside wall of defence was built — fifteen feet thick at the bottom and eighteen inches thick at the top — which today forms part of my garden wall.

A little more than a hundred years later, Sark was plagued by the dastardly scoundrel Eustace Le Moine, the renegade monk who was commissioned by King John in 1205 to recover Normandy which had been reunited to France after 292 years. This Robin Hood of the sea had a gift for leadership and soon united a number of English and Flemish pillage-seekers who rapidly became a formidable band of pirates inflicting horror on the coasts of Normandy and Brittany. Seven years later he threw over his loyalty to King John and offered his services to France, occupying Sark for a time, but John having appointed Philip d'Aubigny as 'Guardian of the Isles', he quickly attacked Sark and took the uncle and brother of Eustace prisoners to Porchester Castle.

In 1216 Eustace again took Sark, but the Islands were returned to Henry III by the King of France, and Henry III gave it to 'His beloved Richard, Vicar of St. Mary's in Sark'. The monks continued their agricultural activities till 1463, when they transferred themselves to Normandy where they founded the Abbey of Montebourg, near Cherbourg, alas completely destroyed by the Allied landings in 1944.

Nothing now remains to record the long occupation of Sark by the monks except their place names (the bay, a 230-foot drop below their mill, is still called Port du Moulin), the defence walls and their well, marked with a stone cross. All that is left of the original cell of Saint Maglorius from which he directed the building of the monastery is a pile of rocks (many of them water-worn, indicating that they were probably dragged up from the beach), massed at the corner of my garden wall. They say on Sark that these rocks must never be moved away or bad luck will follow. Ultimately the body of Saint Maglorius was stolen from Sark by henchmen of a Norman nobleman, Nivo, who wanted a saint's relics for a shrine in which he was interested at Lehon, in order to be exempted from excommunication. Happily, before he had time to remove the cell, the excommunication order for his wild life as a marauder was renewed. The island remained uninhabited for 120 years after the monks had gone.

Perhaps the spirits of monks and pirates really do haunt Sark. Many people have told me that in certain parts of the island they have a strange feeling that dreadful deeds have taken place. Personally, I have never had any such feeling, probably because all my life I have been too intent on living in the present to be conscious of the past. From earliest childhood, I had heard the islanders' stories of witchcraft, folklore and fairies, but for me Father's companionship was much more interesting than old wives' tales.

As soon as I was old enough to hold a revolver Father taught me how to shoot. He used to toss an old top hat of my grandfather's into the air and was furious if I did not hit it as it fell. I was only eleven when he gave me a .303 Martini rifle and a shotgun to use when I went rabbit-shooting with him. If I wounded a rabbit he insisted that I should kill it myself. This made me so sick that I very soon learnt to shoot straight.

Mother was convinced that I had a steadying influence on Father and encouraged us to spend as much time as possible together, which we were glad to do. But he was often busy dealing with the affairs of the island, sailing round other islands with my mother in his yacht or carrying on feuds with the Church — one of his favourite occupations.

In those days the Church of England service was conducted entirely in French, which made it difficult to find a suitable English parson. The first of the French clergy that I remember was a Monsieur Vermeil, who demonstrated his anti-British feelings by skipping the prayers for Queen Victoria. On these occasions my father would rise in wrath from the family pew which was, of course, the front pew, stamp out of the church and go straight home to write a letter to the Bishop. The Bishop would protest to Monsieur Vermeil and for the next few weeks he would unwillingly read the prayers until . . . he'd skip them again, and again there was the same angry performance from Father.

I was grateful when death removed Monsieur Vermeil, because with him went his daughter, my first governess. Daily, since I was five, she had taught me the rudiments of education, combined with piano lessons. Mademoiselle Vermeil was a fierce little woman with an intense hatred of Germany. She had been at school in Alsace during the 1870 war and it was from her that I learnt to distrust all Germans. She made me say the Lord's Prayer every morning in French before starting lessons, and when I was stumbling through my first piano pieces she would rap my back with a ruler and once, exasperated with me, slammed down the piano lid on my fingers.

The Reverend Louis Napoleon Seichan, who replaced Monsieur Vermeil, was a law unto himself. If he disliked any parishioner who had died he would refuse to allow the Church pall to be used on the coffin. He once went so far as to take his maidservant to help him pull down a tombstone that had been erected to a man he hated. In English that was not good, he used to announce that the Collection would be for the 'Organist's Fun'.

It was inevitable that Monsieur Seichan and my father would fall foul of each other. After a dramatic quarrel one day, my father, riding a mare with the foal trotting behind, chased the vicar round and round the vicarage garden. For this indignity Monsieur Seichan sued Father, who had to appear before the Sark Court. As Seigneur, he was more or less a dictator, since he had the right of veto in our

Parliament, the Chief Pleas. Nevertheless he was subject to his own laws and found himself 'bound over to keep the peace' by his Séneschal. This episode, which doubtless caused much entertaining gossip on the island, must have embarrassed my mother beyond words.

Father also spent a good deal of time persecuting my governesses, who consequently did not stay long enough for me to form any lasting impression of them. The only settled character in the nursery was Nana. I dimly remember a Miss Pritchard, whose taste in bright mauve and emerald hats infuriated Father so much that he threw them out of the window. There was nothing for her to do but retrieve them from the lead roof of the pantry and take her leave.

Mademoiselle Mathilde Des Essarts was the only governess with whom my father had a truce, perhaps because she took his side against Monsieur Seichan. She was a sensible, gay little French woman, passionately pro-Dreyfus, whereas Monsieur Seichan, the Corsican, was anti. This led to many excitable rows in which Monsieur Seichan would shake his fist and Mademoiselle Mathilde would throw her head up and snort.

One of the recurring exercises set by Mademoiselle was to write letters to the heroes and villains of the Dreyfus case — to Maître Labory to congratulate him on his defence; to Colonel Henry, one of Dreyfus's accusing officers, and to the Commandant-in-the-Woodpile, Esterhazy, deploring their actions.

I followed the Dreyfus case closely in the *Standard*, the chief Conservative newspaper. From the moment I could read well — at eight years old — Father made me read to him, every day, the leading article. If, owing to gales, the boat didn't come for a week, the accumulated papers were doled out one by one on the subsequent days. From the *Standard* I read about Gladstone, Kitchener and Khartoum, and the Battle of Omdurman, at which a Mr. Nicholson, whom I had actually met, was killed. This made a great impression on me.

Soon after Mademoiselle Mathilde left the island we heard that Esterhazy was lying low at one of the hotels in Sark, but nobody would condescend to take any notice of him — not even Monsieur Seichan.

My sister Doris was born when I was seven years old, and Nana looked after her until she married the farm carter and I was freer to do as I liked. Very few other children came to Sark in those days, so I was lonely when Father was away from the island. The crony of my loneliness was our very old cowman, John Hamon, who in his youth had worked in the le Pelley silver mines. I used to follow him around, admiring the squeak-squeak of his stiff corduroy trousers, while he allowed me to help him lead the cows in and stake them out. One of the most peaceful sounds of my childhood was the knocking-in of cow pegs.

Hamon also acted as the local barber and dentist. On Sunday mornings he would don his best Guernesys, made for him by his wife, with his initials knitted into the side, and proceed to the farm-yard outside the forge. There he attended to people whose faces were swollen by toothache. Each one would be seated ritually on a barrel and held firmly by an assistant while John produced a formidable-looking instrument and yanked the offending tooth out. I enjoyed watching this performance and was not in the least upset by the yells of the patients, although when any of the farm animals were killed I would shut myself up in the nursery and cry bitterly.

On Mondays when the trippers came to see the gardens, I enter-tained myself by climbing to the top of the large arch of the entrance gate, hiding in the ivy and making ghostly noises to puzzle them. While I waited among the dusty-smelling leaves for my next victim I would study the Collings coat of arms over the gate — a horse's head with the motto *Fidelis in Omnibus* — and ponder what fate had befallen this so fondly commemorated horse who once pulled an om-nibus.

Always inventive, I harnessed a pair of goats to a miniature ma-hogany phaeton which had once belonged to one of my great-aunts, and drove along the dusty lanes and cliff paths of the island at a tearing speed. The trouble was that the goats had a habit of coming to a sudden stop and lying down. The only way to make them get up was to pull their hair. Fortunately I was oblivious of their smell.

From the time I could ride Father provided me with a donkey. One of these had a foal who used to come into the house and follow me upstairs. There came a day when the drawing-room tables were laid for a tea party and Tuffy somehow got in among them. By the time the guests were ushered in Tuffy had done her worst. Bread and butter, jam sandwiches and cakes were strewn all over the floor and Tuffy trotted innocently past the startled guests and down into the garden. Both she and I were in disgrace, and Tuffy was forbidden the house. But she had already experienced the joys of gorging on gache, one of the Sark specialities which consists of a dough cake crowded with raisins. Thereafter she took to experimenting gastronomically. This proved the death of her. One day she ate the poisonous berries of *iris foetida*, which grows wild in Sark.

My next donkey had a strange fear of the Coupée. Nothing would induce her to cross it. Although she never hesitated on the narrowest path, she refused to budge from the spot where she could see the 240-foot drop on either side, even when she was blindfolded. I have never heard of a horse that would refuse to cross and some of the islanders concluded that my donkey must be sensitive to the presence of Tchico.

Many people who suffer from vertigo will not cross the Coupée even now that we have put rails on either side. There was a sensible man of Little Sark who used to visit a pub on Great Sark and on his way home would first try walking the length of an old George III cannon which lies on the cliff nearby, to test his sobriety. If it was doubtful, he would lie down and sleep off his excesses beside the gun. There is only one recorded instance of anyone being killed by falling over the side of the Coupée, and that was two hundred years ago, when a man carrying a bale of straw in a gale was caught by a ferocious gust and blown over.

Although I lived an enterprising, boyish life, my nursery routine was very strict and regular. Meals were severely plain and solid. I had to eat four thick pieces of bread and butter at tea before I was allowed jam or cake.

Baths (in a tub in front of the fire) were allowed once a week. There were only a few inches of water which, because it had to be carried by one of the four women servants, by the time it was brought upstairs had become lukewarm.

We went regularly to church on Sundays. Later, my father encouraged me to argue with him on anything we had heard in the service. To support his own arguments on the Gospels he would produce a Greek Testament saying, 'Now I will give you the correct version.' Or if any Old Testament discussion was on, then Josephus was the reference. He hated Nonconformists. 'Their sheep have no wool,' he would say, and could support his claim, because he knew the sheep's wool tithes which were paid to him annually.

For social life we depended a great deal on visitors to the island. Mr. Crofts, who came first when I was ten, was an annual visitor eagerly anticipated and much loved by me. He had been a winner of the Diamond Sculls and was a typical rowing man, tall and powerfully built. We used to go swimming together and, although I never remember a time when I was not able to swim, my confidence in the water was due to his example. It was he who set me swimming problems in tricky tides. Had it not been for him I might not have been able to qualify for my life-saving certificate when I grew up. We used to explore the caves which can only be reached from the sea. He died as he would have wished — drowned one rough morning when he had gone down to bathe — and is buried in Sark.

Frederick Waugh came to Sark and later dedicated a book of reproductions of his famous pictures from the most important United States galleries to me and 'to the memory of Sark where I learned to paint the sea'. There were several other Americans in those days and I remember being taken by Mother to admire a new American baby in its cradle. Making no attempt to conceal my disappointment, I cried indignantly, 'Oh! I thought it would be black and it's just an ordinary white baby.'

A visitor who did not disappoint me was the very dark ex-Queen Liliuokalani of the Sandwich Islands (as we then called Hawaii), whom I admired for her height and her colour. She had been driven from her kingdom in a revolution organised by the American Minister, and had come to Jersey for her exile.

Father was the first Seigneur to remain in Sark the whole year round and not spend winters in Guernsey. But we paid frequent visits there, to stay with my great-uncle and great-aunt Mary Ann — the one my grandfather had wanted to marry. Her face was so masculine that she looked like a female impersonator, and her hair, worn *á la* Lady Blessington, did little to improve her looks. Her side-curls were dressed with macassar oil, against which antimacassars were invented to protect the headrests of chairs. She sternly disapproved of bicycling and used to call me 'Miss' when she was angry. She would say: 'Mark my words, Miss, you will grow deformed and bow-legged from this ridiculous riding.' Great-uncle was a veteran of the Indian Mutiny and had been at Lucknow. I remember the grim thrill of opening a drawer and finding it full of relics of children's blood-stained clothing and locks of hair.

This household seemed intensely old to me. I slept in a large four-poster bed which had red rep curtains with heavy black fringes, and was forbidden to open my windows at night for fear the air would make me deaf. Our once-a-week bath was a tin one raised from the ground like a soup plate and ornamented with painted vine leaves and tendrils. We had sherry and biscuits at noon, and dinner at four o'clock. The valuable old Waterford glass and Sèvres china was in everyday use, but was not destined to survive intact because it was constantly being knocked off the table by the old servant, who was nearly blind.

As I grew older, my Guernsey visits became gayer. There was always some regiment stationed in the island, socially reinforced by a collection of Gunners, Sappers and Naval officers. We would go for

moonlight picnics on bicycles to one of the bays while our chaper-
ones drove sedately down in carriages to join us. There we would
catch sand-eels, which when fried tasted just like whitebait, or go
ormering. In the spring and autumn when our great tides take the
sea down thirty-five or forty feet you can prise ormers off the rocks
with hooks. They have an oval-shaped shell like a small-sized abalone
from the Pacific, and when properly done by an island-born cook
they are utterly, uniquely delicious.

After these nocturnal excursions we would cycle home in pairs
and often 'get lost' to the scandal and secret delight of the Mrs.
Grundys.

Though I was much younger than my companions, life with Father had made me extremely sophisticated for my age. The time he
abandoned me at Cherbourg was an example of my having to deal
with a situation like a grown-up. I was barely fourteen, and off with
Father on one of his frequent yachting trips. Since his boat had no
auxiliary engine we were at the mercy of head winds, or lack of wind.
On this occasion we were obliged to put into Cherbourg, driven
there by a gale. Father took rooms for us at an hotel and then disappeared. There was no sign of him for days and although the owner
of the hotel, Madame Zoppi, was exceedingly kind to me, I grew first
impatient and eventually desperate.

A report came at last that my father had been sighted at Carteret.
So, borrowing the fare from the kindly Madame Zoppi, I set out by
train and horse-bus to search for him. At Carteret there was no sign
of him. I had no money left. Seeing A M Y over the door of a shop
and recognizing it as a Jersey name, I marched in boldly and told the
shopkeeper my story. Believing me, he lent me money to take a little
steamer which ran between Carteret and Jersey though he was not,
as it turned out, a Jersey man after all, but a stolid Norman. In Jersey
a friend of my mother's, a Mrs. Hawksford, put me up, and after a
short stay I sailed for Sark. Since in those days there was no telephone
between the Islands, Mother knew nothing of my adventures until I
was safely home.

In our house the greatest entertainment of the year was in October for the Harvest Home, and we gave a special dinner for the men. The room was decorated with sheaves of corn, flags and hydrangeas. About fourteen people sat down to a meal of boiled mutton, roast beef, plum duff and some sort of milk pudding, Father presiding and the doctor at the other end of the table. After the dinner the women servants burst in, giggling, for the dancing to the music of a concertina. The men took part in the broomstick dance. Two of them, holding a broomstick between them at arm's length, would throw their legs agilely over it and stamp in rhythm to the music. The evening came to an end with everyone roaring 'Mon Beau Marin', 'Madeleine', and 'Auprès de ma Blonde'.

In 1895, there was a rebellion against a law passed by the Chief Pleas proclaiming a close season for rabbits from February to July. Ricks and barns were burnt in revenge against the farmers who had passed the law. Father, determined that there should be no damage on our farm, rigged up a Heath Robinson system of wires and alarm bells. There was no electricity then, of course, so the wires were attached to bells that would ring inside his bedroom window. When the warning tinkled he would wake me up and we would sally out in dressing-gowns with our revolvers. One night we caught a rebel skulking under a hedge. Father seized him, threw him on top of the thorny hedge and sat on him.

Then, as now, I could speak the island *patois* — a mediaeval French incomprehensible to any but the Channel Islanders. My parents, perturbed that this was affecting my accent in real French, which I spoke equally fluently, decided to send me to school in France.

So at fourteen I was despatched to the Sacré Coeur convent at Tours, the strictest of that Order in the whole of France, and the most exclusive. All pupils, before they could be accepted, were required to have the requisite number of quarterings in their armorial bearings.

The journey between Sark and Tours was not easy in those days. I travelled by the old steamer *Courier* from Guernsey to St. Malo in charge of Captain Whales. There a nun of the Sacré Coeur swept me up with monosyllabic efficiency and took me by train for one night to her convent at Rennes. Next morning another nun came from the school to escort me on the long all-day railway journey to Marmoutiers.

The old Abbey of Marmoutiers stands outside the city of Tours, a steep cliff behind it and the lush landscape of the farmlands and vineyards of the Loire in front. This was school: scrubbed refectory tables, coffee in bowls, plentiful food (though for me and the other two English girls too much garlic and too many snails; frogs' legs, however, could be treated as merely tasteless chicken), too much praying and a rigorous accent on modesty. For the rare baths we were allowed, we were given a sort of tented wrap and told to remember that our guardian angel was a man and always watching over us.

After a childhood with my wild father it was difficult for me to accept school restrictions or the Sacré Coeur idea of recreation: no games except hopscotch, modest rambles along the banks of the Loire within sight of the shepherding nuns, solemnly organised visits to the near-by chateaux, and, the only Babylonian diversion, a conducted expedition to taste the new vintage of Vouvray.

On the site of the school there had once stood the church from which Tristan the Hermit preached the First Crusade. Here, centuries later, exasperated nuns preached humility, obedience and the other Christian virtues to a rebellious, lame young girl from Sark. The cliff behind the Abbey was honeycombed with grottoes once used as cells by pilgrims on the road to Rome and the Holy Land, and there, as penance for sliding down the lovely flat polished banisters or for dipping our modesty robes in the bath and dropping them on the floor or for some other defiant exploit, I and the girls I had led into mischief were sent to kneel on the rough-hewn stone floor. Unrepentant before the altars of St Bride, St Patrick or St Samson, and unable to kneel evenly, I would shift uncomfortably from one knee to another for hours at a time, and plan the next gesture against authority.

I handled the inevitable show-down before the Reverend Mother with equanimity. I pointed out to her sagely that the disciplinary psychology of the school was wrong. If, for instance, there were no nun lying in wait at the foot of the stairs to pounce on us for punishment when we slid down the banisters, what would be the challenge? Where would be the thrill? Much impressed, the Reverend Mother experimented with my suggestion. We said we were sorry and did it no more. After that I was not reprimanded, nor did much to deserve reprimand, and was only brought before the Reverend Mother once again, and that was for my mispronunciation of the words 'Rome' and 'Ecureuil'.

Although Father was afraid that I might become a Catholic, Mother insisted that I should attend all the services in the school chapel (the first was at six a.m. and there were others throughout the day) until, as she knew I would, I became saturated with prayer and in revolt from religion. In the holidays, to extract the last remnants of any latent fervour the nuns might have engendered, Father made me read Josephus and Gibbon, and when the Bishop visited Sark I refused to be confirmed.

After two terms I was removed from the Sacré Coeur where I had, on the whole, been very happy. My mother and father met me at St. Malo on the way home and took me to stay at Mont St. Michel — isolated in those days at high tide, with the old causeway under water, and after dark the people carrying lanterns up and down the steep streets. There in the vaulted kitchens, brass pots glittering through the charcoal smoke, Madame Poulard herself taught me to make an omelette. You never washed the pan, otherwise, she maintained, the omelette would stick and burn. A slight flavouring of garlic — apart from that there was no real secret.

But I never liked cooking — I much preferred the dairy. The cows in Sark were always pure-bred Guernseys. Their cream forms too rich a curd to be any good for making hard cheese, but our cream and butter are like none other in the world — a glorious golden yellow. Our dairyman churned it twice a week and I helped work up the butter and shape it into pats. This custom came from the law which ordered every farmer to emboss his sign on each pat, thus making him responsible for the quality of his butter and its correct weight. I have known the finer points of a Guernsey cow and all our crops and their seasons ever since I can remember.

So I returned from school to share a governess with my sister Doris, then only eight. I felt it was rather an insult and implored to be sent away to school again, but Father wanted me at home, and that was where I stayed.

Someone once said, 'There is no need for women to be clever' — a comforting thought for my sister and myself, considering the small amount of education we got.

CHAPTER 3

DAUGHTER VERSUS FATHER

My birthday falls in January and my fifteenth birthday was most unhappy because by now I was conscious of my lameness in a different way and dreaded the impact it might make on men. During the previous summer when crossing to and from Guernsey I had noticed that people sitting on deck would glance up as I walked by, then quickly drop their eyes. Since my short leg had never hampered me in any way and no one on the island had ever seemed to notice it, it came as a tremendous blow to find that strangers regarded me as a cripple. The realisation was insufferable. Night after night I buried my face in the pillow and sobbed for the pleasures which I would never have a chance to enjoy — sobbing with despair and indignation that fate had treated me so unfairly.

Had I still been at boarding school with girls of my own age there would have been less time to brood over the future, but Sark in winter is a lonely place for young people without companions of their own age. The hotels close at the end of summer, and the boat service is cut down to three days a week. There was no telephone on the island and radio had not been dreamed of. We were completely cut off from the rest of the world except on the days when a boat arrived in our small harbour with mail, newspapers and extra provisions.

The winter dragged on. When lessons were finished I went out climbing over the cliffs by myself and thought of all the fun other girls would have when their schooldays were over. They could look forward to gay romances, flirtations, proposals from young men, and marriage, while I was doomed to be an old maid; it was too much to hope that any man would fall in love with a girl who limped.

At last sheer misery galvanized me into working out a constructive plan for the future. I decided that as romance and marriage were out of the question I must train myself to be as useful as possible in the world. The best way to start would be by making myself indispensable to Father. This could be done by writing his letters, checking farm accounts and becoming familiar with the island affairs. Once my mind was made up and I had a definite goal in view, I more or less forgot my handicap and the less I thought about it the less important it seemed to be.

It was about this time that Horatio Bottomley had the idea that there was a great deal of money to be made out of Sark if he could lay hands on it. He offered Father £30,000 for the island — a very large sum of money in those days. This offer seemed fantastic to me and I asked, 'What use would the island be to Mr. Bottomley, and how on earth does he think he can make a fortune out of it?'

Father explained, 'He has calculated that he can start a casino here and make such a profit that he will be able to get out before public opinion is aroused and causes the Privy Council to legislate to close it down.'

As it happened, nothing came of the proposition, which was just as well considering Bottomley's later colourful and nefarious deals.

The next would-be purchaser was Athelstan Riley, a most distinguished member of the High Church, whose one worldly ambition was to become Seigneur of Sark. It was my mother who put an end to that scheme. With great politeness and firmness she informed the worthy gentleman that it was quite useless for him to try to induce Father to sell because she would never agree to it, and went on to explain that by our law a wife has the right of refusing to agree to a sale — moreover, she can retain for her own use and occupation one-third of the house, outbuildings, garden and farm during her lifetime. This is our legal form of The Married Women's Property Act, which it pre-dated by many years, making it quite impossible for an erring husband to cut out his wife. As we also allow no divorce it is a most effective law.

After this interview the subject was closed for good and all. Athelstan Riley gave up the idea of becoming Seigneur of Sark and made his home in Jersey.

By now winter was behind us. A soft warmth poured over the island and spring was in the air, bringing the delicious faint fragrance of wild flowers and sweet-scented gorse. The high rocky ground that slopes down to the steep road from Bel Air to the harbour was gay with flowers. Butterflies fluttered in the gardens and above the deep narrow footpaths winding along the edges of the island. The fishing boats put out to sea again and boatloads of trippers arrived each day from Guernsey.

For me the summer was made all the more delightful by a young man who was reading for Cambridge. We became friends, and when he could get away from his tutor and I from my governess we went climbing and swimming. I introduced him to the grottoes and caves. After a while our friendship developed in a very youthful and romantic way, which made me realise how silly I had been to worry about my limp.

It was on a fine, breezy day in October, when I was sent down in the dog-cart to meet my new governess at the harbour, that I first laid eyes on Dudley Beaumont. He had decided in a most casual way to come to Sark with his friend, Cecil Hayter, a black-and-white artist who often visited the island. Intrigued by the other's description of Sark, Dudley had agreed to come along. There were few tourists arriving from Guernsey at that time of the year and when Dudley saw me standing on the extreme end of the pier as the boat edged its way into the old Creux Harbour he said, 'I would like to paint that girl.'

The reply was, 'You haven't a hope — she is the daughter of the Seigneur.'

Cecil Hayter knew Sark well and on a previous visit had made friends with Mrs. Judkins, an amateur in water-colours, a charming old lady who wore her curly white hair cut short and drove about the island like Queen Victoria in a bath-chair which looked like a sort of chaise, drawn by a donkey. My mother was devoted to her and she lived in Rose Cottage next to the Vicarage.

If anyone could persuade my mother to allow Dudley to paint a miniature of me it would be Mrs. Judkins. Cecil Hayter took him to call on her. In a short time Dudley had met Mother and received an invitation to the Seigneurie. He followed up this visit with so much charm that he quickly induced Mother to let me sit for him, which was the last thing I wanted to do. The sittings bored me to distraction. They did not get me off my lessons with the new governess and, worse still, they prevented me from going out riding and amusing myself in my own way. I soon discovered that miniature painting requires a great many sittings. Half hoping to make Dudley look a fool, I invited him to come out climbing with me, trying him out on our most precipitous cliffs. Rather to my disappointment he came up to my standard, but even so this attractive-looking, slim young man did not impress me at the time. He had a slight stammer, which admittedly he managed very well by dropping the first letter of any word he found difficult to say.

On leaving Sark he wrote me constantly and sent me many books. He knew what kind I liked and chose them with great care. With so much to read, life was made more interesting for me through that dull winter, only enlivened by occasional visits to Guernsey. One of these resulted in my completely losing my nerve in a ship, a fear which has lasted all my life.

It was a stormy day, but I wanted to go over to Guernsey for a dance. I set off quite happily in the little steamer *Alert*. When we reached the west side of Sark we ran into very rough seas and seemed to make little headway. Then we met a really terrible squall off the dangerous island of Jethou. The ship stopped and rolled helplessly on the heavy swell, each roll bringing us nearer to the rocks of Jethou and making it obvious that we were out of control. I knew all too well how dangerous these waters were. My grandfather and grandmother, as I have said, had been wrecked off the reef between Herm and Jethou, one of the former Seigneurs had been drowned within sight of Sark, and there had been any number of wrecks off the Channel Islands. Clinging to the deck rail and paralysed with fear, I waited for the moment when we would strike a rock.

At last a small tug came out from Guernsey and towed us in. Fortunately in those days when many large sailing ships came to Guernsey with coal and timber a tug was always ready to go out. On arrival I found my aunt ill in bed, and my uncle went off to his club before I had a chance to tell him of my escape, so there was no one to talk to. Sitting alone at supper, and afterwards by the fire, it was impossible to take my mind off the terrifying experience I had just been through. The night was one of nightmare dreams.

Since that day I have never been able to overcome my fear of the sea. Its relentless strength and weight and cruelty have become an obsession — so much so that I have seriously considered trying hypnotism to cure myself. Although I have crossed both the Atlantic and Indian Oceans several times I have never felt happy at sea. I love swimming, I have no fear when I am in the water, but I am an utter coward on it. Only the knowledge of what courage I need to go on a voyage makes me unashamed of admitting my cowardice.

A year had gone by since Dudley had left Sark. I considered myself quite grown up at sixteen and a half and had been in England since July visiting a friend of Mother's. The son of the house was paying me a great deal of attention, which added to my enjoyment. I was flattered because he was older and, in my opinion, much more a man of the world than Dudley. It was a surprise when Mother wrote saying she had invited Dudley to stay and had asked him to meet me at Waterloo and escort me home. Two days later a letter arrived from Dudley telling me of the invitation, but adding that before he accepted he wanted me to realise that he hoped to marry me. 'Please think it over seriously,' he wrote, 'and try to look at me in a new light before I come to Sark.' I thought it over and decided that it would be silly to make a decision one way or the other and it was unfair to expect me to do so. Here was a situation that called for tact, I told myself, and wrote what seemed to me a most diplomatic letter telling him to come because I wanted to see him again after such a long absence and get to know him better. Then I deliberately missed the train at Waterloo so as to arrive in Sark a day later.

After spending every day and all day long with each other for a month I decided that after all I did want to marry Dudley. We talked to Mother, who was very sympathetic but said she felt it was too soon and insisted we must wait until after my seventeenth birthday in January before saying anything to Father who, she felt sure, would make many difficulties. Dudley said miserably, 'It is wonderful for me to know that we have your approval but I can't help being disappointed. I had so hoped—'

'I know you are disappointed, Dudley, but you must admit Sibyl is too young to be engaged. Come back and stay with us next Easter. By that time you will both have had a chance to make up your minds and be certain that you really do want to marry.'

'My mind is made up. It has been for a long time.'

'Yes, so it seems, but it is only fair that you should give Sibyl a few months more to be sure of herself.'

He agreed reluctantly and we had to content ourselves with long letters through the winter.

When Mother tried to prepare the way with Father there was a stormy scene and I was given a wretched time. At last I was summoned to the study. Here he announced angrily, 'I have no intention of considering this idiotic proposal until are you eighteen. Get that into your head. I refuse to listen to any more argument, but as your mother has already invited the young man for Easter it would be making this silly business look too important if he was put off, so he can come.'

After that visit Father's fury boiled over. Living in the house with him was a nightmare to me and a misery to Mother, who began to look ill with worry.

Looking back I am not sure that I was really in love, but all this opposition made me determined to get away and marry. The situation went from bad to worse. Almost every day I was shouted at to come into the study where I had to listen to long tirades of abuse and a forecast of all the awful things that would happen to me if I continued to be so 'infatuated' with Dudley. Books would be seized off the table and hurled at me as I tried to escape out of the door.

Finally the day came when I lost my temper. There was the usual shout of, 'Come into the study at once.' I went in, slammed the door behind me, stood with my back to it and said in a very loud voice that shook with rage, 'Stop shouting at me, I'm not standing for any more of this; I've been bullied enough and I won't put up with insults any more. You don't care about anyone but yourself and you don't mind who suffers as long as you get your way. It doesn't matter to me; sooner or later I will escape from you; but Mother can't because — well, because she loves you. And you behave abominably in front of her.' The stored up anger of years against his treatment of Mother came out in a torrent of words. I was in such a towering rage that I hardly noticed his look of astonishment. At last he shouted, 'You're a damned virago.' There was a slight pause and he added with smug satisfaction, 'But all the same you're a chip off the old block,' and I sailed out of the room in triumph.

My triumph was not to last long. Three weeks later Father came into my room about midnight, dragged me out of bed and downstairs in my night-gown, and without saying a word opened the front door and threw me out of the house.

For the first and only time I suddenly felt afraid of him. I fled up the drive and across fields till I had put a safe distance between me and the house. Then I hid in a hedge. Waves of fear swept through me. What could I do? How could I escape? Where could I go for help? The island was so small that I was bound to be found. If this had happened during the day I could have gone to one of the hotels or somebody's house without causing a scandal, but I could not appear in the middle of the night wearing nothing but a night-gown.

Did Father know that Dudley was still on the island staying with friends? I must keep away from him at all costs. My thoughts went round in circles and it was some time before I realised how cold I was. My teeth were chattering and the rough ground had torn at my bare feet. The island was wrapped in a chill mist that blurred the nearby trees and under the hedge the earth felt damp and clammy; but it was a hiding place and I stayed there.

It was somewhere near dawn when the sound of footsteps reached me; two men were walking along the road, and one of them must have caught sight of my white night-dress. The steps halted and Dudley's voice called quietly, 'Come out, Sibyl. It's all right — your mother sent word asking us to look for you and take you to Mrs. Judkins. She says you will be safe there and Mrs. Judkins is expecting you.' So Mother had found out and arranged everything for me. The relief was so overwhelming that I was unable to say a word. The three of us walked silently up the road to Rose Cottage where Mrs. Judkins greeted me with a cheerful, 'My dear, you must be half frozen — come upstairs at once. I have already made up the bed for you.' Without more ado she led me upstairs, handed me a night-gown of her own, tucked me into bed surrounded with hot-waterbottles and made me drink a glass of hot milk well laced with whisky.

I slept for hours and was only woken up by the bright sunlight streaming into the room at high noon. Meantime Mrs. Judkins had managed to get a message to Mother telling her that I had been found. When I woke up Mother was there with my day clothes wrapped in a small parcel. She said I must go away at once and went on to give me careful instructions: 'You must go down to the harbour without being seen and get on the boat as soon as the passengers from Guernsey have landed. You will have to tell the captain more or less what has happened and say that I want you to be away for the time being. He has seen your father in one of his rages and he will understand.'

'What am I to do in Guernsey?'

'Stay away from your aunt and uncle, and board the boat for Southampton, then take the train to London and go straight to your grandfather. I have written out two telegrams, one to your grandfather, which I want you to send as soon as you get to Guernsey, and the other to your father's relatives in Somerset, which you must send off as soon as you reach London. And here are two letters, one for your grandfather, which will explain why I have sent you to him, and the other to Somerset saying you are in need of care and protection. You will need money. Here it is and I have packed a case for you which will be sent to the harbour with passenger luggage from the Dixcart Hotel. It's not labelled, but you will find it in the Guernsey boat.'

'How about Dudley?' I asked.

'I wish he could go with you, but that would look like an elopement and cause a lot of talk. He had better stay on here till the end of his visit and then go over to England. You can be married in London.' She was silent for a moment and then said very seriously, 'Are you quite certain that you want to marry him, Sibyl?'

'Yes, now I am quite certain.'

Mother glanced at the clock on the mantelpiece and stood up. 'If I stay any longer your father will miss me. I had better be getting home.'

Suddenly I noticed how tired she looked and, forgetting my own problems, asked anxiously, 'What will happen to you? Will you be all right? Will Father—?'

Seeing my panic-stricken expression Mother laughed for the first time. 'Don't be a goose, Sibyl. Your father won't throw me out of the house. He may not realise it, but he really is devoted to me. He will be very angry but we all know his temper. It will take a long time before he forgives you for wanting to marry a very nice and perfectly suitable young man, but you must try to remember that, in his opinion, no man has a right to take you away from home.' She kissed me and before I had a chance to say anything more the front door closed behind her.

That day, while Father was hunting for me all over the island on a mare, I made my way safely down to the harbour, following hedges and byways, and slipped on to the boat about half an hour before it was due to leave. I explained all that was necessary to the captain, who had known Father for many years. He was most understanding and helpful. 'Now don't you worry, Miss Collings — just go and hide yourself in my cabin, and leave the rest to me.'

I had hardly got into the captain's cabin when Father rode into the harbour and came on board. He was at once headed off by the captain, who invited him into the bar for a drink while I crouched in the cabin in an agony of suspense. How many drinks were required to keep Father occupied for the next half-hour will never be known, but when sailing time came he was coaxed away over the gangway just in time.

All Mother's instructions went according to plan. First I stayed with Father's relations in a quiet country place called Bawdrip in Somerset where he did not think of enquiring for me. After that I went to stay with an old friend of Mother's in London and collected a very modest trousseau. It was from her house that I was married two months after leaving Sark.

When Dudley and I went to obtain the licence for our marriage we produced a letter from Mother giving her consent. As I was only seventeen parental consent was necessary, but no difficulties were made because it was assumed that Mother was a widow.

We were married at St. James's, Piccadilly. I had sent Father a telegram beforehand to tell him the news. Mother's father gave me away, and as we walked up the aisle I was conscious of a cold prickling feeling at the back of my neck. I thought it quite possible that Father would burst into the church with a gun because I knew he had arrived in England the previous day. The service began, but the words did not penetrate to my mind until I heard the clergyman say,

'Therefore if any man can show any just cause why they may not lawfully be joined together, let him now speak, or else hereafter forever hold his peace.' There was an awful pause. I held my breath and felt my knees shaking, but there was no angry shout of protest.

Although Mother was in England we persuaded her to keep away from the church. Father might never have forgiven her if she had been present.

Shortly after we were married Dudley discovered that I had never been confirmed. This omission shocked him a good deal. So I was confirmed at the very same church in which I had been married a few weeks previously, wearing my wedding dress for the occasion. This, I think, must be a record.

Father apparently had a fixed objection to any daughter of his wishing to leave home. My sister Doris had an equally exciting time when she wanted to marry. She was locked up in her room and shots were fired through the window into the ceiling. During a lull she escaped by sliding down sheets knotted together and hung out of the window. The sheets were part of our grandmother's trousseau and were dated 1844, but they held fast and proved a credit to those who had woven the linen sixty years before. Doris also got safely away and was married in Gibraltar to Captain Henry Verschoyle.

CHAPTER 4

MARRIAGE AND THE FIRST WORLD WAR

I found that I had married into an immense family of aunts, uncles and cousins. My mother-in-law was one of nine Irish sisters, all
famous for their beauty. She at once tried to dominate me, which
she probably thought would be easy as I was only seventeen years
old, but after several wordy battles she abandoned her efforts and
referred to me as 'that Channel Island termagant'. She herself was
one of the seventeen children of James Cooper of Cooper Hill, near
Limerick. Robert Graves, whose father had married another of the
beautiful daughters, describes them in his book, *Goodbye to All That*,
as a haunted family, and tells this story: 'When Cromwell came to
Ireland and ravaged the country, Moira O'Brien, the last surviving
member of the Clan O'Brien, who were paramount chiefs of the
country around Limerick, came to him one day with: 'General, you
have killed my father and my uncles, my husband, and my brothers,
I am left as the sole heiress of their lands. Do you intend to confiscate
them?' Cromwell is said to have been struck by her magnificent presence and to have answered that this had certainly been his intention,
but that she could keep her lands on condition that she married one
of his officers. And so the officers of the regiment which had hunted
down the O'Briens were invited to take a pack of cards and cut for
the privilege of marrying Moira and succeeding to the estate. The
winner was one Ensign Cooper, and a few weeks after marriage
Moira found herself pregnant. Convinced that it was a male heir, as
indeed it proved, she kicked her husband to death.'

On his father's side Dudley was a great-grandson of Barber Beaumont, the founder of the County Fire Office in 1807, from whom
he inherited two widely different interests — miniature painting and
Territorial service. Great-grandfather Beaumont had exhibited no

fewer than fifty-three miniatures at the Royal Academy and was appointed miniature painter to William IV. He raised the first independent Rifle Corps in 1803, known as the 'Duke of Cumberland's Sharp-Shooters', and had such faith in their marksmanship that he once held a target for twelve of them to shoot at from a distance of 150 yards. For many years a stone in Hyde Park, marked with the initials D.C. SS. commemorated the spot where this William Tell-like performance took place.

Dudley's interest in Territorials was encouraged by his uncle, Sir Ronald Lane, a great friend of Lord Roberts and an equally keen advocate of National Service in England.

My first baby, a girl, was born a year after my marriage. The news of her birth was telegraphed to her grandfather, who had refused to have any communication with me since I ran away from home. His reaction to the 'happy event' was a curt telegram which read: 'Sorry it is a vixen.' Nevertheless, I suspect it was the advent of 'baby vixen' (whom we named Amice) that softened his heart, because a few months later we were reconciled. Father actually told me that Dudley was too good for me and it was all my fault, which struck me as a highly *Alice in Wonderland* remark. Exactly one year after Amice was born I had a son. His name was Lionel, but we always called him Buster.

During the first years of our marriage we lived in the Forest of Dean where Dudley had a company of the 2/VB Gloucester Regiment and I met Sir Charles Dilke, also an enthusiastic supporter of National Service. The National Service League was formed at this time and I remember being so impressed by a speech made by him that I agreed to speak for the League myself. Sir Charles seemed to think that I would be an asset because as a Channel Islander I had been accustomed all my life to compulsory militia service. Not only did I speak from platforms, but I also toured the country in a series of National Service League playlets modelled on *An Englishman's Home*. Although this play had been a success it must be admitted that to hundreds of people it was a huge joke and its pompous

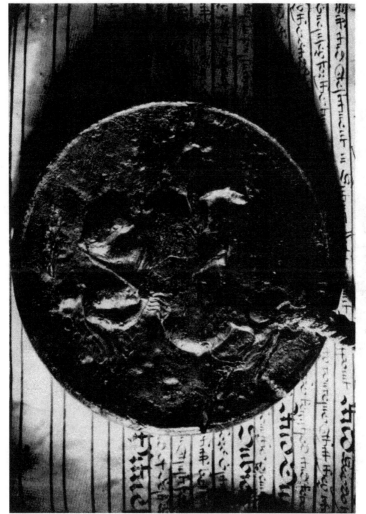

One of the old Royal Charters

The old Stark costume, now rarely worn

The Coupée: a drawing by Turner

Dudley Beaumont

patriotism caused a good deal of merriment. The public speaking and acting was good experience for me and led to all sorts of undertakings later on in my life.

My first visit to the House of Commons was with Sir Charles in 1903, Where I was the interested onlooker on a terrific Irish night when Tim Healy and John Redmond were at their most impassioned and theatrical, with sheets of paper flying around. Many years after, on a Mediterranean cruise in 1927, Mr. Healy, then Governor of Eire, gave me a book in which he wrote: 'From the Governor of one island to the Governor of another.' He also asked me to visit him at Phoenix Park next time I came to Ireland, but I was unable to do so because I was staying with a dyed-in-the-wool, loyal ex-British officer who, keeping a stiff upper lip, informed me clearly that 'no one from this house can visit that rebel.'

Shortly after my marriage I was given a Benz car, which I believe must have been one of the first to be bought in England. In those days it was not necessary to have a driving licence and my car was certainly no danger on the road. It was like a dog-cart with a tiller steering and two projecting handles from the pillar for gear-changing (it had no reverse) and was belt-driven. I always took a large tin of powdered resin to sprinkle on the belt when it slipped. The engine was started by opening up the back and pulling the belt by hand. Most of my drives ended by being towed home behind a horse at large expense, much to Dudley's annoyance.

I had been married five years and had three children by the time it became obvious that Mother was very seriously ill. The previous year she had undergone an operation in Guernsey, but the trouble had recurred and I persuaded her to come over to England and go with me to see a London specialist.

She left Sark with Father on a beautiful clear day in April in the steamer *Courier*. Off the island of Jethou the *Courier* struck a rock and sank rapidly in seven fathoms of water. There were thirty-nine passengers on board, of whom ten lost their lives. The crew went to work to launch the two lifeboats on the upper deck, but were unable to do so, and passengers who had crowded into them were thrown into the sea as the ship went down. Fortunately there was a very small boat on the lower deck. This was launched by two of the crew together with Father and a Mr. Clarke, by dropping it over the stern. My mother and two other women were helped into it and pushed off rapidly as steam was already coming from the engine-room. This small boat picked up more people from the sea until there were thirteen and no room for more. These were hastily put off on to a rock and the boat went to rescue others from the sea, which by now was breaking over the rock and endangering those on it. At last the tug *Alert* came from Guernsey and took them off and saved any others still floating around.

At the subsequent enquiry the captain was found guilty of negligence. The disaster was mentioned in Parliament and questions were answered by Mr. Lloyd George. The following account of the episode appeared in the London *Daily News*: 'Mr. W. F. Collings, the Seigneur of Sark, who with Mrs. Collings was a passenger on the *Courier*, possibly owes his own and his wife's escape to his long and peculiar experience of the sea and its divers perils. For years past, he has been in the habit of cruising in small yachts between the different Channel Islands. Rain or shine, foul or fair weather, the Seigneur has been constantly afloat on what are probably the most dangerous waters in the world. On more than one occasion he has escaped drowning literally by the skin of his teeth.'

When Mother reached England I was appalled by her appearance. After the specialist examined her he had a private talk with me. He said she only had a few months to live and advised me to take her home to Sark as soon as possible. When I broke the news to Father he was heartbroken and showed her such love and devotion during the last two months before she died that I felt it compensated her for much of the past.

Unfortunately I could not stay long to keep Father company and give him comfort because the three small children and I were just moving from the Forest of Dean to Ross-on-Wye, so that Amice, could go to a kindergarten there. I liked Ross — it was such a pretty old town. We lived at Edde Cross House, which had once been the summer palace of the Bishops of Hereford and had a garden stretching down to the river. Douce, my second daughter, was the only member of the household who ever saw ghosts. As a little girl in the nursery she used to say to her nanny, 'Tell that man to go away.' No one asked her what the man looked like and she did not appear to be in the least frightened by him.

Dudley continued his work with the Territorials. We bought a new car, this time a Gladiator equipped with an Astor engine, and I had to take out a driving licence in Hereford. This was in 1908 when very few women drove cars in the country. The following year I became an enthusiastic member of the Red Cross V.A.D. No. 1 (London) Detachment and insisted on doing some extra work as a paying probationer in a London hospital. V.A.D.s were considered the lowest form of nursing humanity and we were given a rough time by a Scotch sister, but the work provided experience that stood me in good stead later on in Sark.

At the end of 1912 Father became very restive and I was told in confidence by several friends that if I did not wish to see him caught and married to a most unsuitable French woman I had better go back to Sark and try to steer him out of this muddle.

My visit to Sark made me realise that if the future was to be safeguarded, Dudley and I would have to make our home on the island. Father would be less unreliable and less lonely if we lived near him and he would have an added interest in his grandchildren. He had never provided me with a settlement, nor given me a penny; but I was his heir and I loved the island passionately, more than anything or anyone in the world. When the time came I intended to do as much for Sark as my grandfather had done. This was my future and I had no intention of allowing Father to take it away from me.

Dudley was busy organising the formation of the South Herefordshire Tennis and Croquet Club and was most reluctant to leave Ross-on-Wye, but in the end I made him see the necessity and we found a small farm near the Sark lighthouse and settled down to breed Guernsey cattle. There was nothing of the farmer about Dudley. Tall and slim, with his military moustache, he looked exactly what he was at heart — a typical army officer who fitted perfectly into English country life and all it stood for. But he made the best of his new life and after a while became quite interested in our farm.

Since we had decided to go in for cattle breeding, I made up my mind to learn as much as possible about dairy work and took a course at the British Dairy Institute under Miss Emily Little in order to take a British Dairy Institute certificate. The Dairy Institute was a part of the University of Reading and, apart from the dairy side, I found immense interest in the life there among students of many races, some from as far away as South Africa, Brazil, the Argentine and Java.

We had hardly put the farm in Sark into working order when the 1914 war began. Dudley promptly joined the 2/VB Gloucester Regiment and, my V.A.D. training now coming into use, I went over to Stover Park near Newton Abbot, which my sister-in-law, Mrs. Harold St. Maur, had converted into a hospital as an overflow for the less seriously wounded sent on from the Plymouth hospital.

Our first casualties began to pour in after Mons, and as I look back to those days it seems incredible that the makeshift hospital should have worked so well. The staff consisted of one qualified nurse, the rest of us being V.A.D.s. My sister-in-law acted as amateur matron, the quartermaster was a very elderly Red Cross worker and the family butler did the duties of an orderly. We were equipped for twenty patients, and minor operations together with general medical care were provided for by the local doctors from Newton Abbot and Bovey Tracy. Most of our cases could walk and had been shunted on the railways and in transit hospitals to make room for the seriously wounded, so they often reached us with dressings which had not been changed for days, their wounds oozing pus and, as likely as not, full of maggots.

The following year I had to leave the hospital as I was expecting another baby. In the meantime Dudley had gone to the Cameroons and joined the 1st Nigeria Regiment. While I was waiting for the baby in London, I was invited by a friend to help her with running a cosmetic shop off Bond Street which she had been asked to take over so that the owner could drive an ambulance in France. It became a meeting place for all our friends, and the most extraordinary customers came in. I remember an eccentric but endearing woman who claimed to paint portraits under psychic control. She had great success and many of her clients who had lost their husbands and sons professed to recognise their lost ones. Personally, I thought this a macabre way of making a living out of other peoples' tragedies.

One day when I went to see my lawyer, he asked me with some amusement if I had any idea what life was like upstairs over our shop, adding that he was quite sure my husband would not like me to be seen going in and out of the building. At first I could not understand what he was talking about — then I remembered a number of champagne bottles being removed when we arrived early in the morning.

Fortunately, my friend and I left the shop before the upstairs premises were raided by the police for being a haunt of immorality and a gambling resort. Not surprisingly, the shop closed down very soon afterwards.

The Cameroons campaign ended when my third son was six months old and Dudley was invalided home with malaria. He was given a spell of sick leave so we went back to the farm in Sark, which seemed an oasis of quiet. There was one great thrill, when a French sea-plane landed just outside the harbour to bring mail for the Governor of Guernsey, Sir Reginald Hart, V.C., who was enjoying a few days' rest in Sark. He was a rabid teetotaller, and even at weddings seized the opportunity of decrying alcohol. By the time he left Guernsey for good he had begun to realise that this habit of his had not endeared him to the islanders. As he was about to leave the harbour, he pointed to a tall column erected to the memory of a previous Governor and said sadly, 'I fear the Guernsey people will not commemorate me in that way.' The quick retort came from a long-suffering official: 'Cheer up, sir, they will probably build a pub and call it the White Hart.'

I was living in a flat at Whitehall Court during the autumn of 1918 when the Spanish 'flu epidemic began to spread like wildfire through London. The onset of the disease was so sudden that people collapsed in the streets and railway stations, in restaurants, in canteens and offices. Business came almost to a standstill. The shops were nearly empty for want of staff and customers. Half the buses and taxis were without drivers, and nurses were practically unobtainable.

That terrible scourge which spread through the whole world from the spring of 1918 to the spring of 1919 is for the most part forgotten today, and there are not many people of this generation who know anything about it. But the death rate was appalling. Five hundred thousand families in America were mourning their nearest and dearest that autumn. In England and Wales alone one hundred and ninety-eight thousand civilians died.

Of all the great towns in England London suffered the most. On one single day in October 761 deaths occurred there, and the same day thirteen hundred members of the Metropolitan Police Force were confined to bed with the disease. Half the ambulance drivers and attendants were off duty for the same reason.

Armistice Day filled the streets with seething crowds which helped to spread infection. By this time I was laid low and very seriously ill as I was again expecting a child. Dudley came back on compassionate leave from France and reached London on 19 November, when the epidemic was at its peak. Five days later, on the 24th, he died. For me, time and events were telescoped and jumbled together as in a nightmare. The entire block of flats was without staff, and it was impossible to get a nurse until the last hour. Then there was no possibility of arranging for a funeral on a fixed day: the number of deaths in London was so great that it was necessary to wait for a date.

Had it not been for my wonderful Cockney daily I would have broken down completely. The real Londoner has a sympathy and understanding in times of need that show themselves in a way which is far more comforting than mere words, and although I can hardly remember what that little woman looked like I shall never forget her kindness.

Dudley and I had spent the seventeen years of our marriage constantly together. Until the war we were never separated for more than a few weeks at a time. Every detail of our life had been planned together and he was more to me than all my children, fond though I was of them. Now that I had to face having another baby in seven months' time, Father's Spartan upbringing helped to steady me. As a child I had often been told by him that whatever I had to endure might still be worse, and that I was not to make a fuss or talk about worries or health. 'Only the smug and self-centred imagine that other people are interested,' he used to say. 'The rest of us should never discuss such topics.'

After the funeral I returned to Sark to await the birth of my youngest child. She was born seven months after her father's death, at the farm which he and I had made our home and where we had spent the previous summer while he was on leave. I named the baby Jehanne. She is the only one of my children who was born and married in Sark.

Though I recovered physically from Jehanne's birth in a surprisingly short time, mentally I was sick with worry. The income from Dudley's estate in the East End of London was almost nil because of neglect during the war. I found myself with little more than my widow's pension on which to live and support six children. The greatest problem was education for the older children. Amice was seventeen, so I was able to give up her school and concentrate on sending her brother to a crammer in England, whence he entered Cranwell as a cadet. Dudley's aunt, Lady Lane, paid for the education of my second son, but when I asked Dudley's father to help with the expense at Cranwell for the eldest the reply I received was, 'My good soul, I shall soon be dead and then you can dance on my grave.'

I replied, 'That is a singularly unhelpful promise, and I have no wish to dance on your grave. I am much more concerned with the problem of getting Buster through Cranwell.'

I then tried to get help from my own father, but he only reached for the decanter, poured himself another glass of brandy and said angrily: 'You are perfectly capable of taking care of yourself and your children. I brought you up to be independent, and I refuse to allow you to come to me for help at this late date.' Of course he knew that I would manage somehow, and perhaps he thought it would be good for me to get out into the world again and make a new life for myself; which was exactly what he forced me to do.

I gave up the farm in Sark and took a house in Guernsey, where daily education was both cheap and excellent. The rent for the house was low, and by Christmas 1919 we were all happily settled there, surrounded by Father's relations and many friends of mine. At first everything seemed all right, but I soon realised that even now there was not enough money to support my family. So I set to work and managed to let the house at three times the rental I paid and found myself a job in Cologne with the Y.M.C.A., re-organising and index-ing the library for our Occupation troops. This job gave me a billet and I found life so cheap that I settled down with my devoted Eng-lish nanny and the three younger children.

One job led to another and after a while I joined the Rhine Army Dramatic Company at the old Deutsches Theater run by that very charming actor, Esmé Percy. With the money I earned it was possible to employ a German governess for the children, and I myself ac-quired a fluent sort of German of the rather kitchen type which served me well when the German occupation came to Sark years later.

Life on the Rhine was pleasant and easy enough, and, with the mark at 800-1000 to the pound, extremely cheap. Later on when it had no purchasing power the financial situation became more diffi-cult. What happened to the Confederate money after the American Civil War was what eventually happened to the German mark, which went up to 100,000,000 to the pound sterling. This was thought to be the limit, and several officers and men bought as many milliard-mark notes as possible. I am told that a few weeks later it was actually more economical to use one of these notes as a spill than to strike a match. Tram conductors kicked handfuls of marks into the street like the rubbish they were, and the rate altered so quickly that articles in the shops were re-priced twice a day. At first the shop-keepers were not quick enough and by the evening it was possible to change enough shillings into marks to buy everything at half price. By the next morning, however, the shops put up the price to the level of what it should have been the previous evening. Keeping accounts was very awkward. Officers drawing pay had to take a fatigue party with several empty suitcases to bring the company pay from the bank, and account books were a nightmare of noughts.

I was told that the Army cashiers at G.H.Q. had to guess one week what the rate of exchange was likely to be the following week. On one occasion the official forecast was so badly out that the N.A.A.F.I. could actually be persuaded to pay the troops a penny not to drink a glass of beer. This sounds incredible, but the rate for the week had been fixed at ten milliards to a penny, which meant that a sixpenny bottle of beer was on sale for sixty milliard. The soldier paid his sixty milliard, drank his beer, handed back his bottle and received one penny for it, for which in the street he could get seventy milliard, so he had beer inside him and was a pennyworth of milliards richer than before.

Since it was not possible to send Amice to finishing school or give her a chance to enjoy dances and all the fun other girls of her age were enjoying in London, I sent for her to join me in Cologne. As I had married at seventeen and Amice was born a year later, she was only eighteen years my junior and a wonderful companion.

We used to take trips to the Unoccupied Zone of Germany at our own risk. I was frequently warned not to do this, but we never had any trouble until we made an expedition to see the first Passion Play held at Oberammergau since the war. To get there we had to have our ordinary passports with their Military Zone stamps visaed for Bavaria. This was easily arranged, and our rooms were booked in the house of the man who was playing the part of Pontius Pilate. We arrived without any delays and enjoyed the countryside where the wild flowers vied with those in Sark. Everyone we met was charming to us, in fact we were actually escorted on one walk to a shrine up the valley by young Lang, who was taking the part of Christ. It gave one a queer thrill to see the face that had been so expressive in the Crucifixion scene a few hours earlier smiling at us from under a green Tyrolean hat! There were very few English there, but swarms of Americans, whose comments on the play and the people seemed curiously inept.

After three days at Oberammergau we decided to break our journey at Munich on the way back to Cologne, but a French officer we met on the train advised us very strongly not to stay in Munich. Instead, we spent two days at a lovely spot on the Starnberger See, in which mad King Ludwig was drowned.

It was still necessary to spend several hours in Munich before taking the overnight train from there to Cologne; so on arrival we sallied out from the station with the idea of taking a meal in a restaurant, and walked to one which we had been told was quiet and good. At the restaurant there were large notices saying 'No French or Belgians served here'. Amice and I decided we looked very English in our tweeds and brogues and would risk being turned away. Inside the room there were dozens of German officers, all in uniform, a sight which of course we had not seen on the Rhine. Feeling somewhat nervous, we followed the head waiter to a table and had hardly seated ourselves when I was startled by an elegant young officer clicking his heels, bowing from the waist and offering me his chair, which was more comfortable than mine. Amice was scared that we would not be able to get rid of him, but he faded away the moment he found we were not Americans. The meal was served with great courtesy, and we caught our train to Cologne.

It was in the train that our troubles began. The gruff and burly conductor came round, examined our passports and immediately shouted that we had no visas to go out of Bavaria, only to enter it, and that we would have to get fresh visas granted at Munich. I discovered later that this was a money-making arrangement on the part of the Bavarian authorities. After the man left our compartment we thought the fuss was over and fell asleep, only to be roughly woken up at 4 a.m. at Aschaffenburg, where we were taken out of the train with two American women and one young English tourist who had ventured on a bicycle trip, being a keen member of a suburban bicycling club. Since neither the American women nor the Englishman spoke a word of German, I had to translate all that was said to them.

We were marched through the streets to the police station by an inquisitive policeman who led us before a typical tough bullet-headed Bavarian sergeant. Without more ado he had us locked up in the night cells. The reaction of the Americans was one of complete fury against their Consul at Frankfurt, whom they intended to see and haul over the coals. To them it was incredible that American citizens should be treated this way and they were outraged. At 6 a.m. the young policeman came to see if we would like coffee. This, I decided, was no time to be haughty and aloof. I made myself as pleasant as possible to him and persuaded him to take us to a nearby café, where we got steaming coffee, hot rolls and honey. I then invited him to have some with us. He was so inquisitive and full of questions that I assured him I had a house full of children and a husband waiting for me in Cologne, who would be heartbroken if I did not get there soon. At this our policeman suddenly became the soul of chivalry and said that if we would come to the back of the Permit Office with him he would get our passports and obtain visas for Cologne immediately. The Americans refused to give up their journey of wrath to Frankfurt and were left behind. I had given them my address and they had promised to come to Cologne, but though I enquired for days at the hotel they mentioned I never saw them again.

When we reached Cologne we found that trouble had started that morning. The workers from the Humboldt works on the other side of the river had come into the square and were rioting. They capsized some of the trams and killed an unfortunate German policeman, one of the so-called Green Police who were unarmed and utterly unable to cope with the crowd of excited Communist workers. Finally Major Hussey, the British R.T.O. at the railway station, arrived with his two Alsatian dogs and escorted us safely to our billets in the hotel across the square. A little later rioting started again, and from our windows we watched the workers trying to saw through the legs of a bronze statue of the Kaiser which stood at the end of the Hohenzollern Bridge, and set some trams on fire. After a while a few military mounted police appeared and the crowd melted into the darkness.

About this time the Instone Airline began a regular service from Cologne to London and Brussels. I made my first flight on a foggy day in a plane called *City of Chicago*. It was extraordinary how light and fragile these planes were. There was one small window in the roof through which we were supposed to scramble, life-belt and all, in cases of emergency. On one flight Dr. Weldon, the Dean of Durham, a really outsize cleric, was with me, and I remember eyeing the size of the window and resolving that if the push came to the shove I was going to be through the emergency exit first, in case he got stuck.

CHAPTER 5

I BECOME LA DAME

At last, nearly five years after Dudley had died, the Beaumont Estate in the East End of London, which had been completely neglected during the war by my father-in-law, was reconditioned to the satisfaction of the building and sanitary inspectors who seemed to vie with one another in complicating every detail. Shortly after the work was completed, I began to get my income, and by 1923 all the arrears of the war years due from my marriage settlement were paid up. Financial worries were finally at an end — there was no longer any need for me to earn money in order to safeguard my children. Amice was now twenty, Buster had just been gazetted a flying officer in the R.A.P., Astley and Douce were safely at school and I had a marvelous nanny for Tup and Jehanne. For the first time in my life I was free to travel and fulfill a wish I had cherished since I had read *Where Three Empires Meet* at the age of eleven. It was then that I had said to myself, 'Some day, some time, I will get to Kashmir,' and I had kept this determination at the back of my mind even when the prospect seemed as far away and as impossible as a journey into outer space. Now I was at liberty to visit friends in India and see Kashmir, and I began to make plans.

Suddenly the blow fell. A letter arrived from my son's Commanding Officer informing me of Buster's debts, which must be met or he would have to leave the R.A.F. This was the first serious difficulty which I had had to face on account of the behaviour of my sons and since that far off day in 1922 there have been many heartbreaking blows. This older son of mine was a very able young pilot and had been one of the youngest to fly at the Hendon R.A.F. display when he was still only a cadet at Cranwell.

There was nothing for it but to summon up my courage and go and see Sir Geoffrey Salmond, whom I had met once at an R.A.F. ball at Uxbridge. After we had been through the preliminary civilities I told him that I would manage somehow to pay off the debts, and added, 'If I do this, will you help me by getting my son out of the country where he will be away from the crowd of young irresponsibles he is running around with?' Sir Geoffrey was very kind to me. He assured me that he understood my problem but he said it was difficult to send Buster abroad because he was just under age for foreign service.

Another thought occurred to me. 'It must cost the country quite a sum to train a good pilot and surely it must be worthwhile doing something to keep him in the Service?' It was not to be expected that Sir Geoffrey would commit himself on this point but I suspected that he agreed with me, and although no promise was made I returned home with a feeling that in spite of officialdom something would be done to help me.

It was not long after this that Buster was astonished and delighted to find himself on the list for Iraq, where he had extra pay allowances and was soon able to make good. Convinced all was now well with my family, I accepted invitations to visit friends in India, and sailed in August 1924. There were not many passengers on board but among them was the fantastic Mrs. Annie Besant with her protégé, Krishnamurti. Mrs. Besant was already famous as a theosophist and an early advocate of birth control, about which she had published a paper jointly with Charles Bradlaugh. This alone shocked the great British public, but worse still was her championship of home rule for India, which made her unpopular with the English and a detestable figure in the eyes of the three Rajahs and their suites who were also on board. She was a large fat woman of seventy-seven, and one fine morning, while she was taking a nap in her deck-chair, a facetious young subaltern hung a 'Not Wanted on Voyage' label over the back of her chair, which really expressed everyone's feelings. Although both she and her protégé were shunned on board, when the ship docked at Bombay Mrs. Besant had a most spectacular reception by her followers. Any number of garlands were placed around her neck and the dock was deep in marigolds and other flowers.

Mrs. Besant and the young Indian were a strangely assorted pair. Two years after my trip to India, Mrs. Besant travelled widely in India and America with Krishnamurti as the new Messiah, urging his claims more vehemently than he wished. Returning to India, she was involved in a lawsuit with the father of the boy and withdrew much of what she had said. She was a strong-minded and opinionated woman, and not in the least put out by the fact that both she and her companion were socially unacceptable on board ship.

One of the visits I enjoyed most in India was to friends in Bihar, who owned a wonderful old estate of the 'John Company' days and belonged to a delightful family called Fraser who had owned it continually, the elder son remaining in the Scottish home and the second son coming out to run the large jute-growing estate. There was a glorious avenue of mahogany trees, the bungalow itself was old and beautiful, lined with mahogany panels, and there was a deep thatched veranda, supported by pillars, which overlooked an artificial lake made over a hundred years ago by slaves on the estate. My visit coincided with that of my host's mother, who was welcomed like a royal matriarch by all the workers, who greeted her everywhere with deep salaams of respect and admiration, and brought her offerings of flowers, fruit and vegetables.

I sailed for home at the end of May. The wonderful interlude had provided enough enchanting memories to last me a lifetime. Years later, during the 1939-45 war, when Sark was occupied by the Germans and my second husband was deported to a prisoner-of-war camp in Germany, memories of India and Ceylon kept me from becoming unbearably gloomy and despondent through the long winter evenings when the only light available came from a small fire in my sitting-room, and after the sundown curfew I sat alone with my worries.

By the time I got back to England, Buster had returned from Iraq and was engaged to a charming girl named Enid Ripley, and Amice

had become engaged to Captain Harry Cantan of the Duke of Cornwall's Light Infantry, stationed in Guernsey. England seemed very
humdrum and unromantic after the glamour of India, and I was glad
to go home to Guernsey with a new car which I had bought in London.

As soon as I was settled in my own house, I began commuting
regularly between Guernsey and Sark. During my absence, Father
had changed so much it was hard to believe that this gentle, placid,
affectionate old man had ever shouted in rage, hurled books at my
head, and dragged me from my bed at midnight and thrown me out
of the house. His fiery temperament had added a spice of adventure
to our companionship, and it was this companionship and his way
of bringing me up which had formed my character. He had given me
the enthusiasm which enabled me to enjoy life to the full and face
bad times without the inconvenience of self-pity. I was touched to
discover that he treasured every letter that I had written to him on
my travels and, as we sat quietly in his sitting-room while he asked
me for news of my children, I felt a nostalgic longing to hear his voice
once more raised in furious argument. But it was not to be. He was
now seventy-five, and had been Seigneur of Sark for forty-five years.
Although he was still interested in the affairs of the island, he found
it too much effort to attend meetings and the Chief Pleas.

A new interest was added to life in Guernsey when Sir Charles
Sackville-West (later Lord Sackville) came to Guernsey as Governor.
An old house called The Mount, which had once belonged to my
great-great-grandfather, John Allaire, had been bought for Government House, and was supposed to be haunted by a victim of my
ancestor's proverbial callousness. The story went that the ghost was
an old woman who had gone one day to implore mercy for her son
who had been accused of sheep-stealing. John Allaire and his boon
companions were carousing in an upper room, and when she appeared to plead for her son they pushed her down the stairs and her
neck was broken. In the eerie watches of moonless nights, her body
could be heard bumping from stair to stair. Apart from the ghost,
there was an ominous superstition that if the driveway gates were

ever closed the head of the family at the house would die. Lord Sackville had the staircase demolished and the drive gates removed. On either side of the entrance he placed two sentry boxes, and a bottle of wine was secretly buried on the spot to remove the spell.

The year 1926 saw Buster's marriage celebrated in London, and a few weeks later Amice was married in Guernsey. In those days there was no airport in Guernsey, so the wedding had to be celebrated at 8 a.m., a slightly grim hour, on a cold winter's morning. The service was followed by a breakfast — in the true sense of the word — attended by the Governor and all our close friends. Then came the send-off at the harbour, and the young couple boarding the mailboat at 10 a.m. Father was not well enough to attend and it was fated that he should die just five months before the birth of his two great-grandchildren at the end of the following year.

At this time we had an exceedingly unreliable doctor on the island, who suddenly appeared in my father's room with his hat on his head and a tall, forked stick in his hand. Nurse registered surprise, and I asked the doctor why he carried a stick, to which he replied, in a thick voice, 'I use it for killing snakes.' Catching sight of the nurse's face, I said, 'But there are no snakes in Sark.' Whereupon he lurched across the room to me and, waving his finger close to my face, said in a very patronizing voice, 'So they say, but I know better.'

It was early one morning when Father's cook, finding him unconscious, immediately telephoned me. I came over from Guernsey at once, bringing a nurse with me, but he died some twelve hours later without regaining consciousness.

The people of Sark genuinely mourned Father's death. He had always been kind and considerate to them and never hard on those who found difficulty in paying their rents or dues. Not only was there real regret when he died but, to a certain extent, some dread and speculation as to what sort of Seigneur I would be.

My first act was to call a special meeting of the Chief Pleas, which consists of the Sénéschal, who presides, the Prévôt or Sheriff, the

Greffier or Clerk of the Court, and the Constable. The first three are appointed by the Seigneur and the last is elected every year by the Chief Pleas. There are forty 'Tenant' members who are all owners of farms and, since the Constitution of 1922, twelve deputies elected every three years by the inhabitants other than the Tenants.

At this first meeting, I made the following speech to the members:

'Messieurs les Tenants et habitants de Serke, je désire vous remercier tous pour votre sympathie envers moi et pour le respect et l'affection que vous avez témoignés pour la mémoire de mon pére. Je n'ignore pas qu'en devenant Dame de Serk je me charge d'une grande responsabilité. Je ne suis qu'une famme parmi vous, mais de coeur je suis un 'vrai Serquais' et avec l'aide de Dieu je ferai tout man possible pour le bien et la prospérité de l'île.

Je me tiens à la disposition de tous. Toute personne ayant de quoi se plaindre n'a qu' à venir à la Seigneurie m'en parler. Je vous promets de vous écouter tous, et de n' être influencée par personne. J' agirai selon ma propre conscience. J' espère que je recevrai toujours votre assistance et votre bonne volonté, et je souhaite la faveur du Roi et la considération de ses représentants.'

And I have reason to feel I have kept the promises I made that day.

The first item on the agenda concerned the doctor; the Court was cleared, several members gave me details of his unsatisfactory behaviour, and it was unanimously decided to replace him. Then followed the discussion of a project to build a new harbour. It was decided to engage a firm of engineers to prepare a plan. For many years this scheme was worked on, and it was finally financed and completed in 1949 at a cost of £52,000.

As soon as I moved into the Seigneurie I set about putting my home in order. There was an immense amount of repair work to be done on the house, which had not been redecorated since my mother died twenty years before. There were no bathrooms and the plumbing was archaic — in fact hardly existed at all. There was not even a sink or tap and all the water had to be carried from an outside pump.

Studying the sixteenth-century walls, some of which are six feet thick, was discouraging, but as the water poured down every time it rained I decided that I would begin by removing the ugly, ornate tower built by my grandfather in 1860. I called in a builder from Guernsey and asked him to demolish it, but the estimated cost for doing so was far too high, so I had to content myself by having some of the odd pinnacles and large granite balls removed. I did, however, add extra bathrooms and new plumbing was installed.

The original house had been built in 1565 and inhabited without a break by the le Gros family, who came from Jersey. The first Seigneur, Sir Helier de Carteret, granted one of the best sites to the original le Gros, well watered and sheltered and with ancient walls and buildings out of which he could construct his house, actually part of the original monastery founded in 565. There were two ruined chapels which were made into stables, the high wall was left for shelter and the house built beside it. In the centre of the house, in a cellar, can still be seen a length of rough wall ten feet thick, with the outlines of three arched openings which were no doubt the baking ovens of the monks, but left standing and filled in when the house was built. It seems as if it was rebuilt in 1675 by John le Gros as revealed by the alterations I made, and the sundial on the southwest corner of the house is dated 1685 and has the initials of le Gros and his wife.

In 1732 the windows were altered and enlarged; I have the account for granite slabs from Jersey for this purpose. The chestnut paneling in the bedrooms is of this date, and also the high stone walls surrounding the flower garden.

The two chapels were preserved by le Gros; the granite lintels over some of the windows of these are beveled and notched in the same way as may be seen in primitive church buildings in France, and they were referred to in a charter of 1196. No altar stone, however, has been discovered. One chapel was last used in 1760, when the then Dame of Sark dismissed the chaplain on the grounds of immorality and closed the church at the manoir and imported a new chaplain.

Needless to say, the estimated cost of repairs to the Seigneurie was five times as much as I expected, so I began by reconditioning the stables for my cattle as I had always been interested in our Guernsey herds. I sold the Allaire House and other property in Guernsey in order to accumulate sufficient funds to pay for this as well as improvements to the house.

The revenue from the island itself, which is collected by the Seigneur, is meagre and uncertain. If the harvest is good and the rents on farms are paid punctually, it amounts to about £180 a year maximum. The Seigneur is expected to entertain all V.I.P.s who come to Sark (of late years this has become a large item), to keep the gardens in good order so that they may be visited free of charge one day every week, to subscribe to all local funds and charities. The only revenue he gets is the 'treizième' whenever a property is sold. Sometimes there are no sales for several years, and another time there may be a windfall of up to £600 or £800, but this is not to be depended upon for income, and there are no entertaining allowances such as officials receive in the other Channel Islands.

Many people have imagined that the Seigneur receives part of the revenues of the island, which are some £14,000 a year, mainly derived from the Landing Tax of 1.6d on all adult visitors plus a duty on alcohol and tobacco. In fact he receives no part of this and contributes his share of the 'Taxe Directe', which is a rate levied on all parties for the care and maintenance of the poor.

When I first came into my inheritance, many of my friends tried to dissuade me from embarking on so much expense and pointed out that I would have to face a lonely life with much responsibility, but I had always had a strong love for the island and felt that Fate had decided that my life was to be there. Also my mother had often urged me to do all I could to lift the island from the neglect which Father had tolerated.

For the first eighteen months after I took over I was overwhelmed with work. Quite apart from all the renovations which had to be carried out at the Seigneurie, there was the island business to attend to, which included plans for accumulating funds for the new harbour, a war memorial which had never been erected, and many other projects. I carried a notebook everywhere and kept it beside me so that at any moment, night or day, I could make a note of the things which had to be dealt with. It was a difficult and discouraging task trying to benefit the island after its long spell of neglect, but I was determined to get prosperity, health, education and all the good sides of progress going and yet never let the island lose its real security, which lies in its freedom, character and peaceful sense of well-being.

Great privileges are always accompanied by grave responsibilities, and, ever since I took over, the Seigneurie has been a clearing house of all island controversy. It is open at any time to any inhabitant who wishes to see me, and I sometimes long for the leisure of the 'tired business man'. Discussions take place on subjects which range from whether bathers shall wear bikinis to whether the Chief Pleas shall take stronger measures to prevent infectious diseases attacking our cattle. As we have no motor-cars I use a bicycle to get to meetings during the day, and, although I have not got my own carriage, when visitors come and I wish to take them out and about I hire one of the island's horse-drawn victorias or wagonettes. These go down to the harbour to meet the boats from Guernsey and drive the sight-seers round. There are about twenty of them and some must be at least fifty years old.

CHAPTER 6

A YANKEE SEIGNEUR

Nearly a year went by before the work necessary at the Seigneurie was completed, by which time, 1929, I longed for a break. How wonderful it would be to get away for a few weeks and enjoy a carefree holiday, I thought. But a holiday was out of the question — so or it seemed until Mrs. Lily Speke, a friend of mine then staying in Sark, invited me to go to New York with her at her expense. She overruled all my objections by saying that she had to transact some business in New York and hated the idea of making the trip alone: it would be a kindness on my part to go with her. We would sail in the liner *Olympic*, stay in New York for the inside of a week and then return in the same ship.

As I had never been to America this seemed too good an opportunity to miss. In any case there was nothing much to be doing in Sark at that time of year. There was in consequence no particular reason why I should not get away for a few weeks. After a certain amount of talk I accepted and it was decided we would sail the following week.

I had to collect a few new clothes in London. When I arrived one of my oldest friends, Mona Linton, said she wanted me to meet a charming American named Bob Hathaway. 'You will like him, Sibyl, he is most amusing and will give you letters of introduction to his family who live in New York. Tell me what day you can lunch at the Berkeley and I will ask him too.'

I said, 'There won't be any time before I sail, but thanks all the same.' However, she was so insistent and took such trouble to arrange a meeting that eventually I lunched with her the day before I sailed. The luncheon was a great success and Mona proved right —

I did like Bob Hathaway; he was not only entertaining but seemed determined to make certain that I enjoyed New York. After luncheon we walked to the Western Union Office in Piccadilly where he sent off long and enthusiastic cables to America.

On board next day I found my cabin full of flowers and nearly every day after we sailed I had a wireless message signed 'Bob'. One of these messages informed me that Stewart Hathaway, Bob's elder brother, would meet me when the Olympic docked in New York. Both Stewart and his wife, Helen, met me and overwhelmed me with kindness during my visit.

One of the most interesting people I met in New York was a ninety-year-old cousin of the Hathaways who told me that when she was a girl her letters came to her unstamped and addressed simply 'Miss Mary Stewart, New York'. Her father had been financial adviser to Abraham Lincoln during the Civil War and she had lived to see New York grow from a small town into a fantastic city of skyscrapers. Her descriptions of New York when she was a girl made it almost impossible to believe how greatly a city could have changed during one person's lifetime.

One of the first surprises I got in New York was when a waiter informed me that ladies were not allowed to smoke in the hotel lounge. His manner indicated that only ladies of joy loitering for no good purpose smoked cigarettes in the lounge. I felt tempted to give him a sharp reproof but thought better of it. Prohibition was in full swing at the time. Of course I had heard a good deal about bootleggers and speakeasys but until then I had no idea to what lengths people went for a drink. Men rushed off to someone's office for a secret hoard of whisky between dinner and the theatre and again later before going on to dance. Everyone carried hip-flasks.

During my visit I came to know a good deal about the Hathaways. The family interest was in Appleton's publishing company. Bob's father had been a well-known Wall Street banker or stockbroker and when he died Stewart had carried on the business. Before the United States entered World War I Bob, with half a dozen Yale classmates, joined the Royal Flying Corps, giving his nationality as Canadian and his birthplace as Winnipeg. Later he was sent as instructor to Fort Worth, Texas, where he saw his friend Vernon Castle, the dancer, crash to his death. I discovered that Bob was in England when the war ended and went back to the States for a few months but disagreed so violently with the prohibition laws that he accepted an offer to manage the London branch of Spaldings, the famous sports outfitter and became a naturalised British subject.

Stewart Hathaway obviously enjoyed talking about his younger brother and I was rather surprised to find myself such a willing listener. After all I had only met Bob Hathaway once and, although I had been pleasantly astonished by the flowers and cables, I took it for granted that he was just being kind-hearted in his efforts to make this visit enjoyable for me. I was not unduly surprised when I received more wireless messages during the return voyage and an invitation to dine with Bob the night I returned to London. It was only natural, it seemed to me, that he would want to have first-hand news of his family.

Before the end of dinner that night it had become clear that this tall, lean Yankee was not only an entertaining companion but a very determined man. I am a strong-minded woman, but this time I had met my match.

We dined together every night for three weeks and after what the newspapers described as a 'whirlwind courtship' we were married on Guy Fawkes Day at Marylebone Parish Church and came back to Sark the next day.

It seemed to me that Bob had shown tremendous courage in his choice of a wife. I was forty-three and had six children, two of them already married with babies of their own. I knew Bob loved London and his life there. Yet he was willing to face the prospect of living permanently on a very small island he had never seen and about which he knew next to nothing. His first surprise came when we landed very early in Guernsey and I waved to an old porter on the quayside calling, 'I'll see you on the Sark boat this afternoon.'

An official welcome awaited us in Sark; flags were flying, shots were fired from guns and officials from the Chief Pleas greeted us at the harbour. When the honours had been done we drove to the Seigneurie. I think this must have been the first time Bob had seen a victoria. By then he was wearing a rather stunned expression. Later on in the evening when we were alone he said, 'I never knew the Dame of Sark was such an important person; why, they treated you like royalty.'

'My poor Bob, you've got a shock coming to you. The Seigneur of Sark is a more important person than La Dame. Under our old feudal laws a husband owns everything that his wife possesses and this applies to the lordship of the island. You are Seigneur of Sark *à cause de sa femme*.'

'How can a Yankee be a Seigneur of Sark? And I wish you would stop speaking French. You know perfectly well that I only speak two languages, English and profane.'

'You aren't a Yankee, you are a naturalised British subject.'

Bob said sadly, 'I suppose when my family hear about this they will say it serves me right for taking out British nationality.'

After we had been married for a week or so, we went over to Guernsey for a couple of days, and I took Bob to call on Miss Carey, a great authority on the Channel Islands. She confirmed his worst fears, telling him that he was, in law, responsible for everything I did on the island. There was a wicked glint in her eye as she said, 'I'm not quite certain but I think that if Sibyl commits a murder you will have to hang for it.'

As a youth Bob had spent many vacations on Bailey's Island off the coast of Maine. Island life appealed to him. He was fascinated by our legends, ghost stories and witchcraft, and I told him of two personal experiences for which I can offer no explanation but which may be of interest to both believers and unbelievers in witchcraft.

Many years ago I had a valuable cow to which some accident was always happening, such as nearly choking to death or suddenly going lame or developing a swollen hock for no apparent reason. One day when I went into the stable I found a length of white knitting wool tied around her hock. My cowman told me that I must on no account remove this because the cow had obviously been bewitched and he had found someone with power to unbewitch her. The cow must wear the piece of wool to keep off the evil eye. From that day she had nothing wrong with her and for many years was a valuable asset in my herd.

A still more personal charm was exercised on behalf of my second daughter Douce who, when she was seven years old, suddenly developed a crowd of small warts on her face. I took her to several doctors who prescribed various treatments which proved useless. Finally in despair I sent her to an old man who was reputed to be successful in charming warts away. I have no idea what he did, but the warts disappeared completely and the old man refused any payment. Again I have no explanation, but to me the important part of the story is that the warts disappeared, never to return.

Douce grew up to be a great beauty. She was tall with a lovely figure, dark hair and enormous dark eyes. Her perfect complexion had the texture of a magnolia. She was painted several times by Cadogan Cowper and one of these portraits hangs in the Sydney Art Gallery. She is now a grandmother, living in Sark, but is still outstandingly good-looking.

I have already mentioned that all the old houses, including the Seigneurie, have stone ledges at the base of the chimneys just above the roof and I explained to Bob that these were for the witches to rest on so that they would not come down the chimneys into the house. He remarked that it was a good thing that the Seigneurie had witches' rests because he would hate to see a witch popping out from the chimney while he was having a night-cap of whisky and soda.

There is one very pathetic ghost in Sark, that of a tragic little lady who came to live with her artist husband for a year or two in a lonely rented house on the island. My mother saw her a few times and told me that she had felt sorry for her because she seemed very lonely and afraid of making friends with anyone. Mother said she was a lovely person, but her husband seemed grim and was a recluse. Then the little lady died very suddenly. She was buried and her husband had a most fanciful cross put over her grave. He then left the island, never to be heard of again. In those days there was no law providing for a death certificate or an inquest.

There was something sinister about that cross. It would not stand up for more than a few weeks. I myself have seen it replaced several times. In an effort to steady it long spikes were attached to the base but invariably it would be found lying on the ground after a short time. Eventually it was moved away from the cemetery and today the grave remains unmarked, unornamented and unnamed.

The islanders were convinced that the sad little lady died in un-happy and mysterious circumstances. Many of them claimed that they had seen her ghost walking along the lane leading to the house where her death took place, and it was even asserted that she would lay her hand on the arm of a stranger in an imploring way.

On St. John's day there used to be a delightful custom of driving about the island in charmingly decorated carts and carriages. This practice died out but was revived again after the last war and is still held annually, now re-christened 'The Liberation Day Parade'.

On the island we also hold an annual Horse Show in May. This encourages the owners of horses and carriages who ply for hire with much profit during the tourist season to ensure that the animals and vehicles are in good trim before the season opens. Prizes are given for the best turn-out and the best horses. The Show ends with an amus-ing bare-backed race known as the Sark Derby. Bob enjoyed this sporting event enormously.

He also took an interest in the island's cattle, which are all pedi-gree animals and entered at birth in the Herd Book of Guernsey cat-tle. They are kept tethered in the fields to economise on the pasture and they are very friendly. The wonderful milk and butter they pro-duce is much appreciated by the tourists. Every July we have a cattle

My daughter Jehanne in the old Sark Militia uniform

The Sark Prison

Bob Hathaway and myself shortly after our marriage

The signature of the first German Commandant of Sark

From left to right, Lieut. Müller, Dr. Lanz, Dr. Maass

Show; the judges come from Guernsey and the Lieutenant-Governor of that island attends to present the cups which have been given for many years by the reigning sovereign for the best cow and the best bull. In September there is the Flower and Farm Produce Show which produces some eight hundred entries — a surprising number for such a small population.

Farming and fishing are the main occupations of the island and during the summer the hotels in Sark buy up nearly all the lobsters, fish and farm produce. Out of season the surplus is sent to Guernsey and before winter sets in every fishing boat is pulled ashore to safety from the storms which lash the coast.

Fortunately there is no unemployment in Sark. We have no trade unions. Every man can turn his hand to any trade that comes his way — it may be building, farming, fishing, carpentry or general trading. However it must be admitted that the island relies for its great prosperity on the ever-increasing number of summer visitors and day tourists. During the past few years these have averaged some 28,000 per annum. Perhaps we are now beginning to rely too much on this import trade and are tempted to neglect our farming and fishing, but for which we would have starved during the German occupation.

As Seigneur of Sark, Bob had to attend meetings of the Chief Pleas, but although he paid great attention to all discussions he never voiced an opinion unless it was asked for. Nor did he ever use his right to veto. I sat next to him, explaining any point that he did not understand, translating French when it was used and advising him how to vote.

Sometimes spirited discussions take place in the Chief Pleas, and Bob was delighted by a story I told him of an incident which occurred when my father was Seigneur. A very old, deaf member fell asleep while the meeting was discussing a landing tax of sixpence a head on all tourists and woke up later when the debate was about a bounty for exterminating rats. He was just in time to hear one of the members say that he objected to poison being put down on the land, whereupon he leaped to his feet, still dreaming of tourists, and exclaimed: 'I quite agree with the speaker. I know that they leave gates open and go through the crops, but to use poison is going too far.'

In his quiet unassuming way Bob made friends with the islanders and it was not long before they took his interest in farming and fishing for granted. Whenever he was stopped on the road by an inquisitive visitor he would say most politely, 'I am a stranger here myself,' which was a neat method of avoiding tiresome questions. Twice he was interviewed by American authors who were writing travel books, each of whom wanted to make a chapter about Sark's first American-born Seigneur. Both seemed astonished that Bob wore ordinary country clothes. One noted that the Seigneur disdained pomp and 'leans towards plus fours, tweeds and sartorial simplicity'. The other remarked that 'Bob Hathaway presides in sports coat and slacks over the island's governing body, the Chief Pleas. . . .' It would be interesting to know what they expected Bob to wear.

The year after we were married, Bob's mother came to stay with us. She was a darling and like many grey-haired women I have known she had the energy of a young girl and a delightfully gay manner. Her interest in any new experience was enchanting and she never seemed to get tired.

I had been a little anxious for fear Sark might bore her, but not a bit of it. She enjoyed driving round the island in a victoria and plied Bob with questions.

'What is that odd little square stone building that looks like an outsize mausoleum?' she asked one day.

'That's our jail,' Bob informed her.

'I thought you told me yesterday that crime is unknown on the island.'

'You're right. I did say so, and it's true. The inhabitants of Sark are the most law-abiding in the world. Almost the last time the prison was used was when Sibyl's grandfather was Seigneur and a party of Oxford undergraduates ran wild and ragged the Constable, who promptly put the leader in jail. The young man asked if he could have one of his books and permission was granted, but when the Constable saw that the book was in Latin he said it was a *'livre de majique'*— no doubt he knew about the famous mediaeval Albertus Magnus book of spells and witchcraft, a copy of which still exists in Sark.'

'Do you still have a Constable?'

'Indeed we do,' I said. 'We not only have a Constable but also an unpaid trainee called a Vigntenier, who serves for one year. He is chosen by the Chief Pleas and cannot refuse the job except with a doctor's certificate.'

A few days later Bob's mother remarked that although she had seen the jail she had not set eyes on a hospital and seemed surprised to learn that we did not have one. I explained that we had a resident doctor in Sark and that anyone who was in need of an operation or hospital treatment was transferred to Guernsey. In emergencies, an ambulance boat was sent over. Even today it would be impossible to staff a hospital in Sark and we still use the Guernsey one.

I have never known an epidemic on the island but I told my mother-in-law about a weird experience I had when nursing one of the keepers in the Sark lighthouse, a young chap who was taken desperately ill while on duty. The old head keeper, for whom I had a great admiration, managed to send to our doctor, who contacted me. He said that in his opinion the young keeper had developed cerebro-spinal meningitis, and was unlikely to live through the night. The situation could scarcely have been worse. It was a misty evening which threatened fog and made it impossible for any boat to put out for Guernsey until next morning. As cerebro-spinal meningitis is highly infectious, it was of the utmost importance that the man should be kept isolated until he could be moved to hospital. To add to our difficulties the doctor was worrying about a woman who was expecting her first baby and might require forceps. We had no nurse in Sark and all I could boast of was my training as a V.A.D. Even that was better than nothing, so I told the doctor I would go and promptly set out on my bicycle. The head keeper, hearing my footsteps as I climbed up the lighthouse tower, met me at the top with a look of intense relief. Treading as quietly as possible, he led me over to a bunk where the poor fellow was lying curled up on one side, facing the wall. His head was retracted in a horribly rigid fashion and he was already mildly delirious, muttering to himself. It seemed that he had complained of a headache when he came on duty but did not take it seriously. However, the headache had rapidly become worse and in less than an hour it had become obvious that the man was very seriously ill.

I will never forget that night — the eerie sound of the light turning and the occasional bird dashing against the glass, our fear that the fog would thicken and make it necessary to start up the siren. The slightest sound or touch made our patient twitch convulsively, and we knew that the noise of the siren would provide unthinkable torture. There was nothing to do but watch and wait for the dawn. Every once in a while the head keeper brewed tea and silently handed me a steaming mug. When dawn came, the young man was in a coma with his eyes wide open, and was mercifully unconscious when he was taken off by stretcher, put on a boat and transferred to hospital in Guernsey. Eventually he recovered, and came back to marry a girl in Sark.

One evening, after dinner, conversation turned to the subject of treasure trove and I told the story of a munition ship carrying a valuable cargo of manganese which had been sunk off Sark during the First World War. Much interest was aroused several years later by the arrival of two salvage ships from Italy, the *Artiglio* and the *Rufilio*, to raise the sunken ship. Our fishermen tried to be helpful, indicating the exact spot where the ship had sunk and explaining in great detail the strength of our tides. The Italians replied that they knew their own business best and proceeded to put a diver overboard. Much to their surprise, he was caught by the tide and surfaced in a minute or two a little way from the wreck. It was then decided that a large block of concrete should be sunk near the wreck to act as a 'deadman' or anchor, and the first ship sailed away, leaving the other to carry on. I was at home when a dripping crew of Italians arrived outside my front door. Their ship had capsized as they had swung out the concrete block. Not only had they lost everything, but one of the crew had been drowned. No one in Sark could speak Italian, and there was no Italian Consul in Guernsey. I spent most of the day telephoning the Consulate in London while a kind-hearted widow in Sark took the crew into her home, found them dry clothes which had belonged to her husband, and provided them with a hot meal. And that was the end of that story. The disaster would never have occurred had the Italians followed the advice of our own fishermen.

After Bob's mother had been with us for several weeks, she insisted that we went with her to Baden-Baden where she intended to take the cure. There were two famous hotels at Baden-Baden. The Stephanie, very smart, very up to date, was the first hotel in Europe to have a swing table for motor-cars which enabled them to be turned round. In terms of English hotels, it was the Savoy. We chose Brenner's, which was the equivalent of Brown's.

Brenner's, which has been in the same family for years and years, was a real solid family hotel. Undistinguished in appearance, it had the best chef in Germany — possibly in Europe. The dining-room (one did not call it the restaurant in those days) was large. The wine list looked like a small version of the *Encyclopaedia Britannica*. Then as now, the clientele was almost entirely confined to the aristocracy — Freiherren, Fürsten and Barons. It was situated in the most delightful park planted with elm trees and Black Forest pines, through which brawled the little Oos river. Then as now, it was the quietest hotel on the continent.

Baden-Baden, we quickly discovered, was the only place in Germany where, when calling a waiter, you said 'Kellner' instead of 'Herr Ober'. In spite of the disturbance of World War I, in spite of the devaluation of the mark, in spite of everything, Baden-Baden was determined to remain as it had been in the days of the Kaiser.

At the race meeting (only four days a year) the club enclosure was almost as exclusive as the Royal Enclosure at Ascot. To gain admittance, you had to obtain vouchers which in turn were exchanged for round orange badges with your name written in ink. Prince Hatzfeldt was the president. The paddock was oval, and surrounded by tall old elms. It was (and is) the most attractive racecourse, with the Black Forest in the background and picturesque farms in the foreground.

Nearly fifty years previously a law had been passed forbidding roulette and *chemin de fer*, so the casino with its tall Grecian pillars and geranium-bordered lawn could only be described as a *Kurhaus*. A major attraction was Dr. Dengler's sanatorium. Dr. Dengler, who looked rather like a Red Indian, had the most aristocratic clientele in Europe and had made a fortune by compelling the very rich to go for a walk before breakfast and be in bed by 10 p.m.

Two other pleasant memories of Baden-Baden are the horse-drawn broughams and coachmen in black tall hats with white bands, and the custom that every man introduced to you had to kiss your hand whenever he saw you. You yourself, as the woman, always waited for the man to bow before you acknowledged him.

In spite of the law against gambling, the International Club was in full swing. It was possible to play *chemin de fer* and a form of roulette in which there were only eighteen numbers, instead of the usual thirty-six plus zero. People who gambled there had the extra excitement of knowing that they might be raided at any moment. They never were. The gambling took place in an upper room, and everybody knew everybody, so there was little danger of an informant telling the police. As a matter of fact I doubt whether any action would have been taken even if the police had been notified.

By now I was calling my mother-in-law 'Mother' though, as I had to admit to Bob, she was far more active than any of my own children. The cure seemed, if such a thing were possible, to increase her energy, and before it was complete she planned a strenuous motor trip all through the Black Forest and on to Aix-les-Bains. Here she had half of another cure, which so stimulated her that we dashed on to Switzerland, then undertook a tour of the French chateaux and, finally, returned to Paris where Bob and I were hoping for a rest. But a rest was the last thing Mother intended to have. She insisted on being taken to all the most scandalous night spots in Montmartre.

'Why,' Bob asked in despair, 'do you wish to come to these horrible places?'

Mother retorted briskly, 'To collect stories about Paris night life to liven up the conversation at afternoon bridge parties when 1 get home. For instance when I describe that place we went to last night where all the women—'

Bob interrupted, 'They won't know what you are talking about.'

'They will by the time I have explained it to them,' Mother assured him.

When it was time for her to sail home, we saw her on board, waved her farewell from the quayside and hastily returned to Sark for a much needed rest.

CHAPTER 7

TRAVELS AND AN ISLAND TRAGEDY

It was Emerson who wrote 'Travelling is a fool's paradise' — in my opinion one of the silliest remarks ever made by a pious man. Be that as it may, I had my 'fool's paradise' in 1936 when I traveled east to Burma in May and west to America in October. I had not planned to go to Burma, but a great friend of mine who had gone there for her health sent a cable to say that she had become very ill in Rangoon and begged me to join her and bring her home. Bob made no serious objection. He merely said he disliked the idea of my leaving him for even a few weeks, but in the circumstances he must make the best of it. Then I promptly telephoned London to book a passage. I sailed a few days later.

It was the time of the Italo-Abyssinian War, and the Bibby liner in which I was travelling tied up in the Canal to allow H.M.S. *Enterprise* to pass us, bringing to England the Emperor Haile Selassie and his suite. They were on deck as *Enterprise* moved slowly past, so near that it would have been almost possible to hand a bouquet to the Empress. Many of us felt we should like to do this as a mark of our sympathy.

My friend and I sailed home as soon as she was fit enough to make the voyage and I returned to London just in time to present my youngest daughter Jehanne at the second of the only two Courts held by King Edward VIII. They were the first of the Garden Party Courts that continued for such a long time. It was a sad thought that Jehanne would never see the splendour of an Evening Court. As we walked across the lawns and had tea in an outsize marquee vivid memories of my presentation at an Evening Court came back to me. What an unforgettable sight — hundreds of young girls and older women wearing lovely gowns and family jewels ,the trains of regulation length, the long white gloves, each head surmounted by a cluster of three white feather plumes. The scarlet uniforms glittering with gold thread worn by officers attached to the Household and the uniforms and decorations worn by the Diplomatic Corps all added to the grandeur. After the presentations the Royal party walked through a lane formed by debutantes and their mothers. As they curtseyed, the dipping feathers were like a wave of white surf at the edge of a shore.

Now the men in their morning dress and the women in afternoon finery reminded me of Ascot. I said to Jehanne, 'You would have more fun on Gold Cup day watching a much more colourful Royal procession and the World's best racing.'

'That *would* have been fun; but it's too late now and, Mummy, don't you think we have been here long enough?'

After a considerable wait our hired car appeared and we returned to the hotel.

Next day we went back to Sark. How glad I was to be home again with Bob.

July, August and September passed all too quickly. In October Bob and I sailed for New York, my first visit to America since we married. My American in-laws gave me such a warm-hearted welcome that I have felt completely one of them ever since. Bob's brother Stewart and his wife Helen met us at the dock. Those two had been wonderful to me on my previous visit to New York when I was a stranger to them and now it seemed as if they belonged to me personally.

Bob was devoted to his brother Stewart and it amused me to note that the brothers were utterly unalike both in looks and character. Bob, tall and thin and always ready to fall in with any plans, taking the line of least resistance, was, however, insistent on punctuality: not only did he arrive on time, but slightly ahead of time if possible. Stewart was far more stable, business-like and down-to-earth. He was shorter than Bob and much fairer — always easy and charming, and never punctual. As his mother used to say, he kept her waiting for his birth and had kept everyone else waiting ever since. Helen remained sweetly unruffled. Like my mother-in-law, she had pretty blue eyes, great animation, dressed beautifully, and was very artistic.

As soon as we arrived we were snowed under by invitations, many of which came from people who had visited Sark during the previous few years. In 1932 I had written an article for the *National Geographic* magazine which attracted much attention, so much that a surprising number of people from the States had come to the island after reading my description of it. The Society invited me to Washington, suggesting that I should come out again next year and lecture on Sark and offering to send a photographer at their own expense to make colour slides to illustrate my lecture.

My first experience of a crack American train was when we travelled to Washington on the Congressional Limited. It was far more luxurious than any train I had ever encountered before. The armchairs in the parlour car were 'staggered' and could be swivelled in any direction. Unfortunately smoking was not allowed in them, so Bob took me along to the club car which was full of armchairs and had a bar at one end. Prohibition had ended and drink was no longer a problem. Even in those days American trains were beautifully sprung. They started and stopped without a jolt and the meals served in the dining-cars were excellent.

Washington impressed me as the most beautifully laid-out city I had ever seen and after a very satisfactory meeting at the Geographical Society Bob and I took an hour's drive to see the sights. Mr. and Mrs. Daniel Roper had lent their car and the chauffeur was a knowledgeable character who seemed delighted to show us as much as possible in the time at our disposal. On the streets I noticed more negroes in five minutes than in New York during the previous three days. Compared with New York the red brick houses of Washington looked very squat and we were told that out of the population of 637,000 one-third was coloured.

We dined at the Occidental, which had the slogan: 'Where the Statesmen Dine'. It was wainscoted with black and white oak beams and had a nice chophouse atmosphere. All round the walls were sayings of American statesmen, mostly presidents. The one attributed to Woodrow Wilson read: 'The supreme test of the nations has come. We must all speak together;' rather facetious, I thought; in view of the surroundings. Robert E. Lee's contribution was: 'Controversy of all kinds only serves to continue excitement and passion.' Bob said that this was a typical American banker's remark and it only surprised him that Robert E. Lee did not preface it with 'My thought is . . .' The waiters all looked as though they themselves had once been in supreme charge at the White House. None of them appeared to be under seventy and each wore a dinner jacket with a stiff collar.

Before returning to New York for Christmas we flew to California to visit cousins who took us all over the States from the Ensenada up to San Francisco. We toured the country at a pace that astonished the Americans, who do exactly the same thing in Europe, and their reactions to my inexhaustible enthusiasm for sight-seeing gave me a good deal of amusement.

After far too short a stay in San Francisco we went on to Los Angeles. When we arrived there, 11 December, we had not heard the latest news from England where the crisis over the King and Mrs. Simpson was at its height. While we were lunching with a party at the Brown Derby before going on to see Mr. Zukor at the Paramount Studios everyone in the restaurant was 'shushed' to silence and, to our horrified amazement, out of the loud-speaker came the King's voice making his abdication speech. For a moment it seemed almost as if this was a Hollywood stunt in the worst possible taste. It was beyond belief that our Monarch should have reached such a terrible decision. As a lone Englishwoman in the crowded room I must have been the only person there who, at that time, remembered the words 'By the Grace of God, of Great Britain, Ireland and the British Dominions beyond the seas, King, Defender of the Faith.'

When the speech ended, a famous actress who was sitting next to Bob said, 'How wonderful of him to make such a sacrifice for love,' and tears had somehow managed to run down her cheeks without spoiling her starry eyes or dislodging one speck of mascara. The sight of her filled me with cold fury and I longed to say, 'This is not the time for sentimental claptrap. Don't you realise that you have just heard one man sacrifice the loyalty of millions? Save your celluloid emotions and glycerine tears for a Hollywood epic.' Suddenly she noticed my disgusted stare, her mouth popped wide open, and she hastily changed the subject. Bob caught my eye and gave me a wry smile to remind me that he also was a British subject. By now the rest of the party looked very uncomfortable, and we left as soon as possible.

In the car I realised that it was my duty to send an official message to the new King as from my island. At the same time a cable must be sent to the Seneschal in the absence from home of my husband and myself. Bob searched his pockets and produced a pencil and crumpled scrap of paper. After a few minutes' hard thinking both cables were drafted and we stopped at a post office to send them off. My message to the Seneschal informed him that I had cabled the assurance of deep devotion and loyalty of all the inhabitants of Sark to our new King. This was promptly followed by a resolution of the Chief Pleas to that effect.

After sending the cables we arrived a little late at Mr. Zukor's palatial office to find him also full of what seemed to me maudlin sentiment about 'marrying the one you love'. Before I had a chance to comment, Bob rapped Mr. Zukor's desk smartly with his fist and said, 'Just tell me how you would feel if your highest paid artist walked out without a scruple in the middle of your most costly production?'

The question appeared to startle Mr. Zukor. 'I hadn't looked at it in quite that way,' he stammered.

'Well, that's the way the British Empire feels about it,' Bob announced in a voice that indicated the subject was a most distasteful one, and the conversation switched to films. We were taken round the studios and introduced to some of the stars. After a bad beginning the afternoon turned out to be most interesting.

We flew back to New York. Since no alcohol was allowed on the planes or at the airport a friend had given Bob a small bottle of whisky, which he had put in the pocket of his overcoat. Before we settled in our seats, Bob folded his topcoat neatly and put it on the rack. Sometime later an overwhelming smell of the forbidden drink pervaded the cabin and we discovered that the cork had come out of the bottle and, worse still, we were being bedewed with whisky trickling down from overhead.

The passengers moving up and down the aisle sniffed suspiciously as they passed us by and, although we made every effort to appear unconcerned, we were horribly embarrassed. Bob said bitterly, 'I could put up with the dirty looks if we had saved enough for one drink, but there isn't a drop left.'

'Breathe deeply and you will probably get the same effect,' I suggested, trying to be helpful.

The smell of whisky was still with us when we landed in New York. It was Christmas week and the city was wonderfully floodlit. Christmas trees glistening with spangles and fairy lights were to be seen everywhere, even on the island sites in Wall Street. Along the whole length of Park Avenue a great Christmas tree stood at every block. The effect was breathtaking. In small houses on the outskirts of New York a tree was placed in every front window and the blinds were left up so that the neighbours could look in. The Christmas decorations presented a delightful proof of the goodwill towards men which is characteristic of the United States.

Until this visit I had not seen Bob in his native land or had the opportunity to compare him with other Americans of his kind. When we first married it had surprised me that he never showed a trace of the proverbial American 'hustle' but fitted into the slow pace of life in Sark without apparent difficulty. Now I began to realise that the American businessman did not get through any more than his English counterpart, though he never seemed to have time to relax and talked business through the week-ends to the boredom of his wife and her friends. The vaunted hustle and speed of New Yorkers is exaggerated. They will rush to an appointment and then waste a lot of time in preliminary conversation. It is easy to realise that England could never have maintained its position on the money markets of the world if its bankers and brokers did not think a great deal faster than most Americans.

After a hectic Christmas in New York we went to stay with an old Yale friend of Bob's, Jack Hays-Hammond, at his amazing museum house in Gloucester, Massachusetts.

He might well have boasted that he was the host with the most in his fabulous stately home. A brief description of the place is enough to make your imagination boggle. The outside has a great Norman keep with a moat and drawbridge which leads to an Italian abbey, the roof of which is fifty-eight feet high. Its monastic effect is stressed by a tall episcopal canopied chair and a rose window. What had obviously been a transept or side chapel was used as a cocktail bar, which seemed little short of sacrilege. However, it was not for me to say so. Beyond this was an indoor pool covered by a glass roof from which tropical rain-storms descended on flowering shrubs, creepers and marble tombs with recumbent figures. At the sides of this pool there was a built-in fifteenth-century house which had been transported from near Tours in France. Above was the complete room of Diego Columbus (son of Christopher), which had been brought from Hispaniola complete with a fourteenth-century Italian bed. The dining-room was from Flanders and, for good measure, there were windows from a house of the Knights Templars at Avignon. In addition Jack Hays-Hammond had installed an amazing organ, of his own design, of one thousand pipes built into an eighty-foot tower. Who could wish for more?

On our return to New York and before we sailed, my mother-in-law gave me some charcoal drawings and water-colours of Sark by

Turner which she had discovered in the Anderson Galleries. I knew that Turner had been in the island more than once in 1842, but had no knowledge of these pictures, and was delighted at this farewell present.

By the time we returned to Sark, work had already started on the airport in Guernsey. Although a landing ground had been in use for some time, this was the first airport, and once it was built there was to be a regular air service from England and the Continent — a great convenience.

Sark is so small that it is impossible for us to have an airfield, but planes have landed on the island — the first in 1932, piloted by the Master of Sempill, who flew everywhere in his own Puss-Moth. He had telephoned me early one morning in August to say he was flying to Jersey, asking if he might land on Sark and lunch with us. Of course I was delighted and told him we would make a 'smudge-fire' in our large open field, and hang sheets over the nearby telephone wires. We all dashed out from the Seigneurie, built the fire, hung out the sheets and waited in high excitement. Presently we saw a very small plane against the clear blue sky. While we held our breath it circled and made a perfect landing in the narrow field. Sempill and Jimmy Wentworth Day stepped out of the plane as calmly as if they had driven up in one of our horse carriages. At lunch they told us they were on their way to Jersey to confer with Lady Houston. This was the first of many visits to her preparing the way for the famous flight over Everest which was sponsored by that amazing, eccentric but wonderfully patriotic woman. On succeeding flights to Jersey Lord Sempill made it his business to fly over Sark and drop a bunch of the day's newspapers into my garden. In those days we thought it marvellous to have a newspaper on the day of publication. There was another occasion when Sempill landed and flew off with the ten-day-old calf that I had given him. It had to have its legs put into a sack because the plane was made of nothing heavier than light wood and canvas. Even a baby calf might have kicked a hole in its side.

Three years later I landed on the island from another Puss-Moth, piloted by a young airman named Haig, who flew in from Guernsey. Others who landed here at that time were Denys Tollemache, Michael Montague and my youngest son, who was also a keen aviator. During the war there was a forced landing on the island one night by one of our own planes, and a few years ago I was landed here from a helicopter. But aircraft on Sark are few and far between.

For us in Sark 1938 was a year of comings and goings. The latest craze was for speedboats. All through the summer they sped out across the water from Guernsey and darted round the small islands. Great excitement was caused when some people landed on one of our beaches during a fine sunny day and snatched a child who was playing under the care of a local nanny. The child was on a visit to the island with her English father, who was staying at one of our hotels. Horrified by the sight of her charge being kidnapped in broad daylight, the agitated nurse dashed to the hotel to tell her employer what had happened. He immediately got in touch with our Seneschal, who arrived with the child's father and nanny at the Seigneurie, demanding my urgent assistance.

Having listened to their tale of woe, I telephoned the authorities in Guernsey, and was informed that a party had arrived with a small girl, but that they had already taken off by a chartered aircraft from a temporary airfield. By the time I got through to Scotland Yard on the telephone the party had already landed at Croydon and been detained, so I was able to pass on the news to the child's father. After he had left the Seigneurie with the Sénéschal and the nanny Bob turned to me and remarked with a grin:

'This is the first time I have seen you in the role of a private detective.'

'When you have lived on the island as long as I have you will realise that the Dame of Sark is expected to be a Jack of all trades,' I replied, adding rather smugly, 'As a matter of fact, I think I make rather a good detective.'

A few days later we heard that the child's parents were divorced, and the mother wished to take her daughter to America against court orders, but the father was equally in the wrong because he had no authority to bring the child to Sark, which was outside the jurisdiction of the English courts. All Sark followed with interest the newspaper reports of legal proceedings after this strange case. As divorce is illegal in Sark, the whole affair seemed particularly thrilling to us.

There had already been a most worrying incident which caused me even greater concern than the kidnapping. One morning it was reported to me that on the edge of a rocky cliff there was a pile of clothes that had been seen on the previous afternoon by a party of people going round the island in a boat. Next morning the fisherman who had taken the party on their tour reported to the Constable that the clothes were still there. The Constable enquired at every hotel and lodging-house to ask if anyone was missing, and then came to me as it appeared that all our population was intact.

I telephoned to Guernsey, but there had been no report of any missing persons. However, the police got busy and found two suitcases unclaimed at the left luggage depot on the quayside. Oddly enough, a guest who arrived to stay with me the previous day had noticed a man and woman sitting on deck near him, and remembered they were looking extremely unhappy and holding hands in a far from ecstatic way. I asked my guest if he would look at the clothes that had been found on the rocks, and he was able to identify them as being worn by the two people in question. No return tickets had been forfeited. In the meantime, the Guernsey police had traced the name in an overcoat left in the luggage at Guernsey to a tailor in Chatham. The London press made a great feature of this story and went so far as to put out posters announcing 'Mystery in Sark'. As a result, I was badgered by reporters who had decided that the man had murdered the woman and escaped, and even went so far as to say he had been seen in Guernsey. As boats leaving Sark accounted for all passengers I felt that the couple, or at least the man, must be either drowned or on the island. The Sark fishermen, in whose knowledge of the tides around our coast I have complete faith, assured me that if the couple had been drowned near the rocks where the clothes were found their bodies would not be washed away, but would go round and round and finally rise to the surface nine or ten days later. We also know that a woman's body when drowned comes to the surface before a man's.

A strict watch was kept for the following ten days, and although the reporters persisted in their theory of murder, I held firmly to the evidence of the Sark fishermen. Sure enough, the woman's body came to the surface within a week, but still the rumour of murder persisted. However, after a final and rather acrimonious interview with the reporters I was thankful to announce three days later that the man's body had been brought in, which, all things taken into consideration, seemed to prove a suicide pact. I must in fairness add that one of the reporters, representing the rest, had the grace to come to me and say: 'We have to hand it to you. You were right all along.'

Then during the summer of 1938 a film unit asked permission to come to the island and film scenes from Victor Hugo's *Toiler of the Sea*. My eldest son Buster had financial interests in the venture, a French producer, Monsieur Jean Choux, was in charge, and the leading parts were played by well-known actors and actresses. A small steamer had been bought and altered to fit the period of the play, in order to be wrecked in the scene which Hugo describes so vividly, and we watched the shipwreck, which was most dramatically carried out on one of our best known rocks, the Autelet. Later I saw the part of the film which had been made on Sark and thought it beautiful, but, alas, when the company went to England for the studio scenes there were financial difficulties and the whole project collapsed.

Meantime, I had begun to think seriously about the suggestion which had been made to me in America a few months previously by the National Geographic Society in Washington: that I should prepare a lecture to be given there early the following year. Bob and I had met Lowell Thomas at a dinner party given by the Beecher-Stowes in New York, and during the course of conversation they had mentioned the proposal. Mr. Thomas had said that in his opinion a colour film was essential, even if slides had to be used as well. I told him that my experience as an amateur photographer did not qualify me to make a film. After a few minutes' thought he said:

'The man who could make a superb job of it is Arthur Radclyffe Dugmore. I wrote his life story, *A Rolling Stone*. You may not know it, but he did a lot of pioneer work filming wild animals in Africa.'

Arthur happened to be an old friend of mine, so I wrote to ask him if he would come to Sark and help me. The result was a very successful film. While Arthur was making it I acquired much knowledge of photography, which enabled me to continue throughout the year making detailed pictures of the seasons in Sark and of the occupations of the people at work and play. When Arthur left, the Geographic Society sent a very fine photographer named Anthony B. Stewart to make studies of all the beauty spots, which were made into coloured slides in Washington.

Apart from the invitation to give one lecture to the National Geographic Society I had invitations to lecture in Paris to the Société Géographique and also to the Belgian Geographic Society in Antwerp.

Bob had suggested that I put myself in the hands of a New York agent who might be able to arrange more lectures. To me it seemed unlikely that anything would come of this, but to please Bob I wrote to an agent he knew saying rather grandly that, although I was prepared to give a number of lectures, there was to be at least two nights' rest between each lecture. It was a shock when the agent wrote back promptly, informing me that he had booked nineteen lectures and could have arranged many more had I not made my stipulation.

While all this was going on, Baroness von Hutten, known as Pam, the title of her successful novel, tried to persuade me to write a film story about the island. She was living in Sark at that time and was convinced that I would be able to sell the story because period dress films were popular just then. Fired by her enthusiasm, I began making notes of all the most exciting historical incidents. Before I had got very far with this a French friend of mine came over from Paris to stay with us and was so interested that between us we developed quite a story, introducing a love interest, the theme being made up of the happenings which had occurred in Sark up to 1565. I had not quite finished this story when the time came for Bob and me to go to America, in the early spring of 1939.

As usual before we left the island, Jehanne was given legal authority to act as deputy Dame during our absence. I always have a copy of a document written in French ready to hand to Jehanne when I leave the island, which provides that she shall *'Représenter ma personne et agir comme man député en tous cas de mon absence des Chef Plaids'* and the Seigneur promises to *'avoir pour agréable et tenir ferme tout ce que mon dit député sera fait et passé sur l'obligation de tous mes biens, meubles et héritages.'*

On board the *Queen Mary*, while I was still working on the Sark film story in French, I met a New York publisher who became interested in it and offered me a contract if I would translate the script into English. There was no time to do this because of the lecture tour, which would cut out any possibility of extra work, but my niece, Cynthia Hathaway, undertook the translation, and it duly appeared in book form under the title of *Maid of Sark*. The Turner pictures that had been given me by my mother-in-law were used as illustrations.

My first lecture was in Washington to an audience of over two thousand in the D.A.R. Hall. As zero hour drew nearer, I began to suffer from a bad attack of stage fright.

Bob did his best to boost my morale by saying over and over again: 'It's ridiculous of you to be scared. There is nothing about Sark that you do not know better than anyone else, so for goodness' sake stop worrying.' Although he put on an air of great confidence I suspect that he too was a trifle nervous.

A few days before the lecture we were guests at the Women's Press Club of America and I was asked to speak. The prospect of standing up at the table filled me with alarm, but once I was on my feet confidence came back and I began by telling my audience about a story that had been published in one of the English newspapers shortly after I became Dame of Sark. A printer's error accounted for the fact that the k was left out of knight when stating that I 'held the land from the King for half a night's fee a year'. This story raised a big laugh and broke the ice. After that it was a pleasure to talk to such delightful people.

My lecture tour included a number of colleges, and I was surprised at the students' interest in Sark, its feudal traditions and daily life. For me it was fascinating to compare these young Americans with English boys and girls of the same age. The difference was considerable. Our public school system prepares young men better for life, giving them more maturity and easier good manners than the American counterpart. On the other hand, American college girls had far greater poise and polish than English girls of the same age; though they did ask some rather ridiculous questions such as: 'Do the girls in Sark make up, and do they wear lipstick?' The answer was, 'Yes, of course they use powder and lipstick just as English girls do — in fact, if you met two girls, one from Sark and the other from England, it is unlikely you would be able to tell the difference by looking at them.'

After one lecture in Cleveland I was taken aback when a fashionably dressed woman came up, shook my hand warmly and said: 'I am so glad to meet a real Dame, not the sort my husband knows.' At a loss to know how to acknowledge this compliment gracefully, I merely thanked the lady for her kindness.

In Chicago I was thrown slightly off balance by being asked: 'How do you manage to keep down the population on Sark? Do the people practise birth-control?'

My answer to this one was: 'Honestly I don't know, because I have never asked.'

I had been warned that American audiences were critical, full of questions, and impatient of hesitation in a reply by the lecturer. However, as my lectures were entirely non-controversial I found only genuine interest and enthusiasm everywhere. Certainly some of the questions led me to think that the audiences must have imagined we were some sort of aboriginal race instead of the civilised bi-lingual people that we are — with, thanks be, a good sense of humour for added measure. At the beginning of every lecture, before showing the films and slides used for illustrations, I used to try to convey the atmosphere of the island by saying that the life we lead is entirely different from that in America. No motor-cars, no income tax or death duties or surtax, no unemployment, no trade unions, no politicians. Shops and hotels can sell what they like and when they like except on Sunday, which is strictly a day of rest. Sark is not, however, a sort of feudal pageant to amuse visitors. It is a real live community of people who are happy to have retained their ancient form of government, and possess a subtle dignity of their own, born of many years of independence, honourable work and satisfied old age. We have plenty of compensations for our political system which anyone will tell you was old-fashioned eight hundred years ago.

I had undertaken the lecture tour in the hope that it would bring American visitors to us. This hope was realised, for I constantly find that I am greeted by tourists who stop me to say that they met me after one of the lectures.

As soon as the tour was finished we sailed for home, but left the ship at Cherbourg and went direct to Paris where I lectured at the Salle d'Iéna, in French, to a delightful audience, many of whom have since visited the island.

In Jilly my charming sister-in-law Helen Hathaway and her adopted daughter Valerie came to stay with us. In August I went with them to the other islands and then for a motor tour in England. We visited Stratford-on-Avon and shattered the complacency of the caretaker at Ann Hathaway's cottage when, having signed the visitors' book, we told her that none of us was a Hathaway by birth.

War was then declared before Helen and Valerie could leave, so they had an anxious return voyage in a Dutch liner. During the crossing the *Athenia* with many women and children on board was sunk some distance from them. Personally, I went home to Sark to prepare for war and offer the Seigneurie to the Canadian Government to use for convalescent officers.

CHAPTER 8

THE GERMANS TAKE OVER

All illusions that the Channel Islands were likely to remain immune from the rigours of war were shattered during May and June 1940. The first shock came on 10 May. It was a lovely morning, peaceful and serene, when we turned on the B.B.C. news bulletin expecting to hear nothing more exciting than the humdrum reports to which we had become accustomed during the past nine months of the 'phoney' war. To our astonishment, we heard the announcer's voice informing us that Germany had invaded Holland and Belgium.

There was an uneasy lull, and then the blow fell. On 21 May we listened to the evening news bulletin at six o'clock and heard that the Germans had forced a wedge between the French Army and the B.E.F. Arras, Amiens and Abbeville had been captured. The news, next morning, was awful. The B.E.F. was obviously cut off. More than 350,000 men were in France with, apparently, no means of getting out. The day was almost as dark as night, and all we could hope for was that the torrents of rain would bog the relentless advance of the German tanks.

Then came the epic of Dunkirk; but we were too far away to get first-hand information, and official news bulletins were very guarded. No mention was made of the second B.E.F. force which was sent out to try to hold a line but had to be brought back when the French armies disintegrated. There was an ominous sign, plain for all to see on 9 June, when a dark pall of smoke rose sky-high from the coast of France and cast its shadow over the islands. The French were blowing up oil storage tanks: the enemy would soon be on our own doorstep.

By now French fishing boats were arriving in our harbour almost daily to obtain food and water for those on board who had been able to escape the German onslaught and were making a desperate effort to reach the south coast of France. One of these boats was a lovely yacht, crammed with French families, ranging in age from a grand-mother down to a tiny baby. They had no clothes except those they stood up in, no stores, and no charts of any kind; the reason being that they had jumped on board at Le Havre and stolen the yacht. The navigator was a fisherman who had never sailed these waters, and the engineer was a motor mechanic. My daughter and I provided milk-foods for the baby, and clothes. I even managed to find an old chart of the Brittany coast which had belonged to my father. I often wonder how they fared, but their fate remains a mystery, for we never heard from them again.

Some of those we helped remembered us and sent postcards after the liberation. Heaven alone knows what happened to the others.

The refugees had one thing in common. They all told us tales of the horrors of Occupation likely to create alarm and despondency, for it was apparent that in the very near future we, too, would suffer the same fate.

The French Government had been evacuated, the Maginot Line was overrun and the British Chiefs of Staff decided to recommend to the War Cabinet that the Channel Islands should be demilitarized, as it was obviously impracticable to attempt to defend them. Only a few miles of sea separated them from the French airfields which were now in enemy hands. Masses of German artillery were within easy range, the thickly populated islands could easily be devastated, and the only thing to be done was to send over a sufficient number of ships to Jersey and Guernsey to evacuate those who wished to leave. The official decision came, of course, from the Cabinet, and two let-ters were flown over from London, one of which was delivered to the Lieutenant-Governor in Guernsey and the other to the Lieutenant-Governor in Jersey. Both were identical and written by the Under-Secretary of the Home Office. Each read as follows:

Home Office.

19th June, 1940.

Sir,

I am directed by the Secretary of State to say that, in the event of your recall, it is desired by His Majesty's Government that the Bailiff should discharge the duties of Lieutenant-Governor, which would be confined to civil duties, and that he should stay at his post and administer the government of the Island to the best of his abilities in the interest of the inhabitants, whether or not he is in a position to receive instructions from His Majesty's Government.

The Crown Officers should also remain at their posts.

I am, sir,

Your obedient servant,

A. MAXWELL.

People from Alderney and Sark who wished to leave the islands would have to cross over to Guernsey in order to board the ships sent from England. I went over to Guernsey for the day to find out for myself what was happening there, and was appalled when I saw the panic. The High Street was packed with winding queues of people waiting to draw money from the banks, and their strained faces showed how anxious they were to get away. The State offices were in a state of utter confusion and the only man who appeared cool, calm and collected was the Bailiff's secretary. Having seen what I came to see I boarded the afternoon boat back to Sark and during the crossing made up my mind how best I could protect my own people.

There were many things to be considered. First the inherent character of the Sark people, who are a close-knit community, caring for nothing and nobody outside the island. To these self-reliant, self-confident people, many of whom are direct descendants of the first forty families brought over to protect the island during the reign of Elizabeth I, anyone visiting Sark, even an English tourist, is a foreigner and therefore should be treated as a guest who is entitled to courtesy no matter how tiresome he may be.

Since the fall of France, Bob and I had received frantic telegrams from my family in England and his in America urging us to leave the island. But I was convinced that I must stay with the people and guard their interests to the best of my ability. I felt that in many ways I was qualified to face this crisis. One great advantage was my ability to speak and read German, although it must be admitted that my command of the language was not of the highest standard. As I have said elsewhere I had spent some time in Germany after the First World War and since then had met a sufficient number of Germans to acquire some knowledge of their national characteristics. Moreover, my name and status were included in the Almanac de Gotha, which in those days could be guaranteed to make clear my rights and authority when dealing with upper-class Germans; and if the lower classes made any attempt to bully me or my people I knew full well that neither they nor It would show any signs of cringing.

When I got home that evening I discussed the situation with Bob and together we decided that we had no alternative but to remain on the island and accept our bounden duty, no matter what the consequences might be.

On Sunday evening after church I called a meeting of the inhabitants and told them of our decision to remain with one of my daughters and her small girl, but that transport to England could be arranged for those who wished to leave. In the case of evacuating young children I advised that the parents, or at least one of them, should also go, so that the family would not be broken up, but those with a home and a stake in land should stay, and I went on to say, 'I am not promising you that it will be easy. We may be hungry but we will always have our cattle and crops, our gardens, a few pigs, our sheep and rabbits.'

By a curious coincidence it was thirteen years ago almost to the day since I had made my first speech to the Chief Pleas in June 1927. I had then said, 'I do not ignore the fact that as Dame of Sark I take

Talking to German officers outside the
Seigneurie. My weight at the time was 7 stone 2 lbs.

Hollywood, 1946: with Bob Hope and Bing Crosby

upon myself great responsibilities. I am only a woman among you, but at heart I am a true Serquais, and with the aid of God I will do all in my power for the good of the Island.'

Never had my responsibilities been so great as they were now, and at this time it was impossible to visualize the five weary years ahead, or to foresee that the Occupation would later bring us to a state of semi-starvation.

The result of this meeting was that not one Sark-born person left the island. A certain number of English residents left, and many times during the ardours and endurances of the years which followed I felt terribly weighed down by the burden I had undertaken. Later on, when Bob was deported to a prison camp in Germany, there was no one to whom I could turn for advice. I had to fight for our rights by myself, and I felt a deep affection towards all those people who with courage and self-reliance had followed n1y example and re-mained on Sark. I thank God that in the end our choice was justified. Although many houses were damaged and everyone was hungry, the island was still secure and we were able to pick up the thread of our lives from where the curtain had descended on us in 1940. But I am going ahead too fast.

The British Government had demilitarized the Channel Islands by 20 June, but for some strange reason had delayed in informing the German Government, through its representative power, of this fact. Therefore, it was a shock when on Friday, 28 June, the Germans attacked both Guernsey and Jersey by air.

It was a perfect summer day and Sark was utterly peaceful under a cloudless blue sky until, at six o'clock in the evening, we heard the intermittent drone of German aircraft and went out into the garden to watch three aeroplanes flying low over the island on their way to Guernsey. A few minutes later we heard the ominous explosion of bombs which were being dropped on St. Peter's Port; but we were too far away to hear the machine-guns which fired on civilians in the streets, haymakers in the fields and an ambulance carrying wounded to the hospital. Twenty-three people were killed, five died later and there were many wounded.

Within half an hour the planes flew back over the sea to Sark, swooped down and machine-gunned our small fishing boats around the coast. As luck would have it their aim was faulty and no hit was scored either on the fishermen or their boats. Next day the Germans landed on the Guernsey airfield and took over control of the island. Our telephone was cut and during the next four days we had no way of knowing what was happening in Guernsey. After their recent experience the fishermen dared not expose either their boats or themselves to another attack, so no boats put out to sea, nor did any German boat arrive. There was nothing to do except keep calm and wait in suspense. The unspoken thought uppermost in everybody's mind was, 'What will happen to us when our turn comes?'

At last on 3 July, the old Guernsey lifeboat was sighted heading for Sark. I sent the Seneschal to the harbour to meet the German officers and bring them to the Seigneurie, and then went to the school to reassure the children and some of the women who had read of German brutalities in Poland and were naturally much more alarmed than the children; but by assuming an air of cheerful confidence, which I was far from feeling, I steadied them. It took me less than ten minutes after this to reach home and have a consultation with Bob.

'Let's take a leaf out of Mussolini's book,' I suggested. 'We'll put two chairs behind the desk at the far end of the drawing-room. It is a long room and they'll have to walk the whole length of it, which will give us a certain advantage,' adding, 'Besides, they'll have to walk up those few stairs from the hall and then turn right before they are announced, and that will also help us to look more impressive.'

Bob agreed, and we hastily moved two chairs to the back of a large writing table so that we could face the invaders. Next I sent for my maid.

'Now, when the German officers arrive, announce them, as if it was an ordinary occurrence to have German officers calling on us.' She carried out my orders with great good sense.

I was determined that this island, at least, should show a front of firmness and dignity and give the impression that we were taking everything in our stride in the firm conviction that we would make the best of a bad time which we were convinced would not endure long. I can only say that to my knowledge no sign of defeatism was ever shown in Sark throughout the Occupation.

The Seneschal, who was not a man to be flustered, went down to the harbour at his leisure and met the two German officers who stepped ashore. He informed them that he was there to conduct them to the Seigneurie and that as no motor-cars were allowed on the island they would have to walk. So they climbed the steep hill and trudged along the rough country road until they reached our main gate. There was a scrunch of military boots coming down the drive. Bob and I sat in tense silence till we heard them wiping their boots on the doormat. Turning quickly to Bob, I said in a low voice, 'I know Germans. That is most reassuring. It is a gesture of respect to the house.'

My maid opened the door, asked their names and announced them: 'Major Lanz and Dr. Maass.'

They both wore the drab green uniform of German officers, service dress jacket, breeches, jackboots and forage caps. Both gave the Nazi salute as they entered the room. I fully expected to hear 'Heil Hitler', but I must say here and now that it was never once said in my presence during the five years of Occupation.

Lanz, the Commandant, was a tall, alert, quick-spoken officer, with dark hair and dark eyes. In civilian life he had been a Doctor of both Law and Philosophy, and I believe he came from a family of agricultural machinery manufacturers in Stuttgart. Maass was a Naval surgeon who spoke perfect English and had studied tropical diseases for eight years in Liverpool. There was a difference between these two men which was obvious to me the moment I laid eyes on them. Instinctively I judged Lanz to be a fair-minded man, who would never trick anyone by low cunning, but there was something about Maass which made me distrust him. His face was too smooth for my liking, and I could well imagine that while in England he had sent back a lot of valuable information to Germany which had nothing to do with tropical diseases.

A large printed poster was produced, half in German and half in English, headed 'Orders of the Commandant of the German Forces in the Channel Islands'. Among the orders were a curfew from 11 p.m. to 6 a.m.; all forms of guns, rifles, etc., to be handed in at once; all sales of drinks forbidden and licensed premises to be closed; no assembly in the streets of more than five persons; no boats to leave the harbour without an order from the military authority. We could keep our cameras and wireless sets, but only until the following year.

Lanz spoke no English and Maass was his interpreter. When I had read the notice I turned to Lanz and said in German, 'Please sit down. I will see that these orders are obeyed.' Both men seemed astonished that I could speak their language and Maass said, 'So you can talk German.'

'Badly, but well enough to understand it and to make myself understood.'

Then he gave me a wonderful opportunity by remarking, 'You do not appear to be in the least afraid.'

Looking as innocent as possible I asked in a surprised voice, 'Is there any reason why I should be afraid of German officers?'

This question had an immediate effect. They assured me that I was indeed right in my assumption. Their manners suddenly became most affable and Lanz went so far as to say that if ever I found any difficulties I was to communicate directly with the Commandant of the Channel Islands in Guernsey. I took advantage of this throughout the war, and it paid big dividends. I always went over the head of the local Sark Commandant and I soon discovered that this official had a hearty respect for my contact with the High Command in Guernsey, which put a stop to any petty tyranny by local officers in Sark. When there were new orders which had to be communicated to me I insisted that the Sark Commandant should come to the Seigneurie, and when I had any complaints I never hesitated to voice them. The occupation of the islands by the Germans could have no possible effect on the outcome of the war, but Hitler was so anxious, for reasons of propaganda, to hold British territory that he was prepared to isolate large numbers of men and use much material for this purpose. At that time the Germans were victorious everywhere, sweeping over Europe on the crest of the wave and, as usual with them, keen to make a good impression where people of what they called 'kultur' were concerned.

I was treated with great courtesy by the senior officers and I, in turn, extended to them the hospitality of the Seigneurie which is due to all visitors in this island who are made known to me. It is one of the pleasures and penalties of the Dame of Sark that she never calls on strangers in her own island, but invites them to her home. During the Occupation this feudal etiquette served me well. For instance, in the course of polite conversation I was often able to acquire useful information which would not otherwise have been available and, in an affable manner without argument or rudeness, indicate that we were not much impressed by Hitler's régime or German boasts.

At first we were assured that the war would be over by Christmas, and indeed the Germans had bought up all the English tweeds in Guernsey, which they intended to have made up by English tailors in London. The polite response to this was, 'Of course, no one can deny that English and Scotch tweeds are the best in the world, or that London tailors are vastly superior to those in any other country, but it seems to us rather wishful thinking to assume that the war will be over by Christmas.'

When we were told the Germans would certainly invade England even if it entailed losing a million men, Bob and I voiced some doubts about the success of this venture. These were greeted with smug expressions and indulgent smiles. I made a point of putting banned anti-Fascist books such as *Sawdust Caesar* and *The House that Hitler Built* in a prominent place on my sitting-room bookshelf where they were bound to be seen. It was fun to watch the Germans eyeing them, but I was never asked to move them, which was disappointing because I had planned to say, 'Take them away by all means. Everybody on the island has already read them in any case.'

To begin with, the occupation of the island was entirely military, and all we had on Sark was a sergeant with ten men who took over what they were pleased to call 'military control' on 4 July. As my American husband remarked, 'A hell of a day on which to be occupied.'

The first few months were quiet and uneventful. I was told to carry on the civil administration as usual, and things were made comparatively easy. The mark was fixed at two shillings and one penny, but it had to be remembered that the Germans held all the trump cards, so that when they requisitioned anything it was difficult to refuse. Sometimes I tried to argue but, when it was a 'military necessity', nothing further could be done.

We found out later that the first troops sent to occupy the island were specially picked to impress on the British people that the Germans were well-behaved, well-disciplined and with a kind-hearted. The behaviour and discipline of these troops was excellent, and it was rare to see a drunken German soldier in those early days.

A few days after the Occupation, three young men arrived on the island; two Frenchmen and a Pole, who had somehow managed to acquire a small dinghy and reach Sark without being noticed by the Germans. They were brought to the Seigneurie where they begged me to arrange for their passage to England. The French wanted to join the Free French, and the Pole also wanted to enlist for active service. I had to tell them that with the best will in the world it would be impossible for them to leave Sark and reach England. It was hopeless to attempt to reach England from Sark in a dinghy; all the fishing boats were under German surveillance and there was no communication with Guernsey except by a little German boat.

There was nothing for it but to provide them with a meal and advise them to give themselves up. After so much effort to escape they were, of course, bitterly disappointed and I did my best to comfort them. The young Pole told me that he had a small Polish flag which he wore next to his heart, and he would rather die than allow the Germans to take it. So we made a solemn pact. He and I together burned his flag and, although he was clearly heartbroken, he was consoled by the certainty that it would never fall into the hands of the enemy.

Although we never heard from those three young men again I have a feeling that the two French lads probably survived. What fate had in store for the young Pole doesn't bear thinking about and sometimes I wonder if it would have been kinder to let him drown rather than face the horrors of German slave labour; but we knew nothing of that in those days.

With one exception I did not leave Sark during the Occupation because I was afraid that requisitions might be made if I was not there to argue about them. On this particular occasion I had to go because word was brought to me secretly that two British officers had landed in Guernsey from a submarine and were hiding in my daughter's empty house. Amice had closed her house when she left the island to join her husband, who was soldiering in England, and the man left in charge of the place had come over to see me as he had no means of helping them. 'They have no ration cards, so they can't even get food, and I don't know what to do about them.' He also knew, although he did not mention the matter, that if he was found harbouring British officers he was liable to deportation or even death. The islands had been demilitarized only a few weeks before, and yet here were British officers already back to spy out the situation. They were Philip Martel of the Hampshire Regiment and Desmond Mulholland of the Duke of Cornwall's Light Infantry.

I took some tinned supplies and went across to Guernsey on the pretext of being in charge of my daughter's property. The young men were in a desperate plight. Their mission had been to land on Guernsey in plain clothes, spy out the land and guide a Commando raid two nights later. Having done this they were, if possible, to be taken off by submarine. They had followed out their instructions, but nothing had happened — there had been no Commando raid on the expected day, no submarine to take them off and, worse still, by remaining on the island they were exposing their families in Guernsey to the greatest danger. Even though their families were ignorant of their presence, some local might talk and retribution would be bound to follow. Their last remaining hope was that I might be able to arrange for a fishing boat to come from Sark and get them back to England. It was a miserable business having to explain that this proposition had no chance of success because our fishing boats were strictly guarded by the Germans and, apart from that, there was no possibility of getting sufficient petrol for such a venture.

In the end they had to give themselves up, and lucky it was for them that British uniforms had been stolen in which they could surrender. Had they been caught in civilian clothes they would have been shot as spies. Later, members of their families living in Guernsey, who were completely innocent, were deported to France, a punishment typical of the Nazi régime.

But the time had not yet arrived when we were to experience the worst hardships enforced by the Nazis.

CHAPTER 9

OCCUPIERS AND OCCUPIED

The prophecies made to us with such glib confidence by the Germans in July 1940 were not yet fulfilled; the war had not ended by Christmas. The spring of 1941 was the loveliest I have ever known, and it seemed a thousand pities that our friends could not be on the island with us to enjoy it.

In May, unbeknownst to me, all the prominent English newspapers reported that I had been deported to Germany. This report reached America and a reference was made to it in a broadcast on the Radio Newsreel, North American edition, on 20 May. The broadcast announced, 'It would be interesting to know whether any of the islanders attempted to invoke the ancient custom of the "Clameur de Haro" when their ruler was seized by the Nazis. In removing her to a concentration camp in the Reich the Germans have done an extremely foolish thing. La Dame has an authority recognised and respected by the islanders through ties of long custom. To seize her as a hostage for their good behaviour is likely only to stiffen the resistance of a population who have both spirit and *esprit*, who have a stubborn genius for cold-shouldering interlopers, and who have long been accustomed to taking their cue as to hospitality from the attitude of the Seigneurie.'

Reporters in England interviewed Jehanne, who told them that the last messages she had received from me a short time previously gave the family no cause for alarm, and therefore it seemed most unlikely that I had been deported.

Our official newspaper, the Guernsey *Evening Press*, was, of course, controlled by the Germans and forced to publish any announcement that the enemy considered fit to be read by the islanders. Needless to say, the German editorials were angled to un-dermine our morale. There was only one occasion when, quite inad-vertently, they provided the islands with the greatest possible morale-booster, and that was on 23 July 1941 when the most important news on the front page was in a heavily lined box editorial. The im-posing headline read, 'V German Victories on All Fronts'. The news story announced, 'The whole of Europe is impressed by the unique propaganda campaign which all believe is the symbol of uniting hun-dreds of thousands of people with the German people, their unity expressed by the letter V, the initial of victory.'

And in heavily leaded type, *'Viktoria.'*

'The sign of the certainty of German victory in the struggle for Europe is also a sign for THOSE WHOSE COLOURS HAVE NEVER BORNE A RETREAT BUT ONLY VICTORIES. *V is the sign worn displayed with the certain confidence of a German victory on all fronts.'* There followed an ecstatic reference to V-signs which were worn in Paris and all Occupied countries. In their pompous reference to 'those whose colours have never borne a retreat but only victories' the Germans seemed to have forgotten that they had suffered defeat in 1918. The Occupied countries knew full well that the V-sign was instituted by Churchill and was displayed in all the countries which had been overrun. It was hilariously funny to read the official Ger-man version.

Towards the end of that summer aerial activity had increased, and in September the Battle of Britain, which was intended to knock out the R.A.F. before the invasion, had been won, but not by the Luft-waffe. England had not been invaded, although the blitz was in full swing. No one doubted that the German claims of punishment in-flicted on London night after night were justified, even if exagger-ated, and we knew that London was not the only city being blitzed. Of course, we only heard the German side of these grim bulletins; the English reports were strictly censored.

By now our quiet existence had changed. We had been warned that the military authorities would turn over their administration to civil officials and that conditions would then deteriorate. The warning was justified — conditions did deteriorate. Instead of one sergeant and ten men, we were now bedeviled by swarms of officials who arrived and demanded statistics of every conceivable kind. These men had no military bearing. In spite of the uniforms they wore, they were nothing more than jumped-up peace-time clerks and office workers. Financially, they were most assiduous, demanding constant balance sheets of the island's finances, which must include an 'estimate of future revenue'. As we were then paying the cost of maintaining troops on the island, and their numbers varied from week to week, the estimates were quite worthless.

'How do they expect us to work out future estimates under these conditions?' I asked Bob in exasperation.

'Quite simple,' he said easily, 'all we have to do is to think of a number and double it.'

This formula worked like a charm. Our figures were never criticized or verified.

Every day we had to be ready with details of all sorts at a moment's notice. Bob said glumly to our friends, 'The Seigneurie reminds me of the Information Bureau at Grand Central Station.'

Of all of the islands we were in the best position to withstand occupation. We were four hundred people, mostly able to produce vegetables. We had 103 cows, a few rabbits, some of us had poultry and others pigs. The men were either farmers or fishermen, so we had our own crops and our own fish. All had been well until we had been subjected to bureaucratic rules and regulations. The office workers in Army uniform knew no more about farming and fishing than the islanders did about office work, nevertheless they gave numerous instructions as to what crops should be sown and how they should be grown.

If anything could be thought amusing in those days it was the German effort to control our fishing. They were so afraid that fishing boats might escape and reach England that an armed soldier was placed in each boat, in spite of the fact that no boat had enough petrol to make the voyage. The disciplined German mind also proceeded to fix a time of day for fishing. For instance, a notice would be affixed saying, 'Fishing tomorrow will be allowed between 10 a.m. and 3 p.m.' The guards would be waiting at the harbour but the fishermen would not, knowing that at 10 a.m. it would be useless to fish, and being unwilling to waste their precious rationed petrol. The guards reported their absence to the local Commandant, who came to me to complain. I explained over and over again that the success of fishing depended entirely upon the tide, which varied, and the interview always ended with a promise on his part to 'appeal to higher authority to have the time varied'. Whoever this higher authority may have been, it took some time to get it understood that hours, as such, had nothing to do with fishing. In the end comprehension dawned. This point had to be conceded because the Germans needed the fish as much as we did. The Sark fishermen amused themselves by deliberately steering the boats into large waves, watching the German guards getting well soaked and often sea-sick, and staying out much longer than necessary for the pleasure of watching them get sicker and sicker.

Wireless sets were now prohibited but I had hidden one and there was one other concealed on the island. The penalty for discovery was 30,000 marks, which of course no one had, or imprisonment or, in certain cases, death. We hid our set in a trunk left behind by one of our friends who had evacuated. As I had a whole stack of trunks and suitcases of other people's in an empty room, this one among a pile did not arouse suspicion when the Germans searched the house, as they sometimes did. I went to the length of packing it in an old moth-eaten blanket, to which we added moths from time to time. We only dared listen to the 9 p.m. news, and there were four of us, Bob, our farm bailiff Bishop, his wife Jenny, and myself. We had decided on a drill to be carried out if the Germans suddenly came to the front or back door. I had two large poodles who always barked at any sound. If they barked, I was to go slowly down to the door, making a great fuss of quietening the dogs, while the others were putting away the set. My limp would act as a good excuse for my slowness and provide extra time. We were taking a considerable risk, but one which was well worthwhile.

Constant propaganda by the German troops and their newspapers might well have undermined the morale of the islanders, but on an island with only 400 inhabitants news spreads rapidly, and a few words passed on quietly each morning worked wonders. We could meet our neighbours shopping, wait till the right moment occurred, then say, 'The B.B.C. announced last night——' Those to whom information was passed on could be trusted never to admit under any provocation that they had heard it.

The relationship between the Occupier and the Occupied was of the utmost importance, and to me it was a great strain to keep a balance. In the first place, we could do no good by sabotage. There could be no underground movement where there was absolutely no contact with the outside world — we were like prisoners in a gaol with a garden to it. Our only weapon was propaganda, and our only propaganda was a cheerful confidence in victory for the Allies. We never disagreed with the Germans openly, but we could annoy by asking ostensibly silly questions, such as, 'Haven't you landed in England yet?' or 'I suppose Russia has by now been conquered.' I found I could irritate them by asking innocent questions about education in Germany, and when told of Hitler's youth camps expressing great surprise that children could be sent to these without the parents' wishes. This particularly stung the fathers who were Roman Catholics.

Although we listened to the nine o'clock news bulletin from the B.B.C., and we knew that London was being bombed, we did not hear details of the *Blitzkrieg* on other towns, and I had no way of knowing that my eldest son, Buster, had been killed in the Liverpool bombing. He was in the R.A.F., but at the time was on leave and staying in an hotel in Liverpool. My daughter Amice, who was with her husband in England, called at the American Embassy and asked if they could get the news to me, which they were able to do as the

United States was not yet at war. A message was sent via the Berlin Consulate to the Commandant in Guernsey, then to Colonel von Schmettow, Commander-in-Chief of the Channel Islands, quartered in Jersey, to transmit to me, and I must say he showed the greatest kindness and consideration in informing me as gently as possible.

All house telephones had by then been taken away from us, so a message was brought to Bob asking him to go to the Sark Commandant's office, and there he was told the news and asked to break it to me. I appreciated the Commander-in-Chief's kindness, but was quite unprepared for the strange incident which occurred a few days later, when he and his A.D.C. crossed from Guernsey and called at the Seigneurie to express their sympathy.

It was one of the most difficult moments of my life, but I stiffened my spine and made an effort to accept with calmness and dignity the enemy's condolences. Count von Schmettow made it easy for me by saying, 'My sympathy is for mothers of all nations who grieve in the same way for their sons.'

This made good sense to me and I said, 'You are very wise, and I must tell you that I am grateful to you for your kindness and courtesy.'

I discovered that von Schmettow was a nephew of von Rundstedt. He was a German aristocrat and a soldier of the old school. His father had been a personal friend of the Kaiser, and visited him each year in exile at Doorn. Von Schmettow himself joined the cavalry in 1909, had served with the German Army for over thirty years, was wounded on the Eastern Front during the First World War and later lost a lung when gassed on the Western Front, where he commanded an infantry regiment. He was tall and erect and, although he looked dour, was really very kindhearted. He made great efforts to oppose food cuts and to refrain from repressive measures. Two years after Buster was killed, von Schmettow's own son was killed on the Russian front and, feeling that I must repay the courtesy he had offered me in my bereavement, I sent him a card of sympathy.

We had our first taste of the Gestapo when the German doctor in charge of the troops was found early one morning murdered in his bed. The Commandant came at once to interview me and he seemed convinced that the crime had been committed by an islander.

'But the islanders don't murder people; there hasn't been a murder on Sark for hundreds of years,' I protested.

He was not at all impressed by this statement, and left looking extremely grim. Next day news got around that the doctor's batman, whose name was Uhl, was missing and we were accused of harbouring him. A curfew was imposed at 7 p.m. — this, in May and with the early summer-time, meant that we were shut in, from a daylight point of view, at 5 p.m. A special permit had to be obtained from the German Commandant to allow a man to tend his cattle after that hour. For ten days the batman could not be found and every male from sixteen to seventy years of age had to report twice a day to the *Kommandantur*. When the batsman's body was discovered at the bottom of the well at the doctor's house, suspicion was grudgingly lifted from Sark men. In the dead of night Uhl was buried in a desolate spot on the cliff and we heard nothing more of the matter. The well had actually been in use all the time, but apparently without any ill effect. It reminded me of a gruesome verse which went:

> 'Into the well
> That the plumber built her,
> Aunt Eliza fell.
> We *must* buy a filter.'

The story goes that, many months later, the Germans learned that Uhl was innocent but had been so worked on by the Gestapo that he had jumped into the well. The real culprit was a soldier who had been malingering to avoid being sent to the Russian front, whom the doctor had certified as fit to go. He had his revenge by murdering the doctor and had left in the early hours in the draft which embarked before dawn. Later, when the soldier was wounded and dying, he confessed. This story may or may not have been true, but it is true that one dark night a German detachment exhumed Uhl's body and removed it to a consecrated military cemetery in Guernsey.

To begin with, the German doctors were only responsible for the troops. In peace-time the health service on Sark is carried out by the resident doctor. Whenever a doctor leaves the island, it falls to me as chairman of a committee to interview applicants for the post and choose the one best fitted to serve the people. In my opinion, the doctor is the most important member of the community. He must be a good general practitioner willing to take a personal interest in every family and to listen to his patients' problems as well as diagnose their symptoms and provide suitable treatment. An old doctor is not likely to be up-to-date in modern medicine, and a young doctor has no future in Sark — the very fact that he applies for the post indicates that he wants to retire before he has gained worthwhile experience of general practice. The ideal age is in the middle fifties and the right man for the job is extremely hard to come by.

It had been a great blow to me in the summer of 1940 when our resident doctor decided to leave Sark with the English evacuees, and I was at my wits' end to know how to replace him. Eventually, I offered the job to a retired district nurse in Guernsey, who accepted the post and came over to Sark with her husband. As time went on it became obvious that she was going to have a baby, but she still continued working until the baby was due, and it then became my duty to act as midwife. It was a slight shock to both the mother and me when we discovered that I was about to deliver twins. However all went well, and neither the mother nor her babies seemed a penny the worse after my ministrations.

When I got home, Bob asked, 'How did you get on?'

'I would have you know that I have just delivered twins, which is one more than I bargained for.'

'In that case you'd better have a drink.' He filled a glass and handed it to me.

'What I'd better do, Bob, is to apply to von Oettingen and find out if it is possible for the German doctor stationed here to provide medical aid to the civilians.'

Prince Oettingen was in command of civil administration in Guernsey. As soon as he received my appeal, he came over from Guernsey to see me and at once promised to send the Oberstabsarzt to arrange about medical aid, and from that time on throughout the war it was given willingly and unstintingly at any hour by the Army doctor quartered in Sark. These doctors were changed every two months as they were all suspected of being unduly influenced by the islanders.

Prince Oettingen was charming to us. He had travelled a great deal, and we had many mutual friends. Whenever he called on us in Sark it was a pleasure to see him. We could gossip about the people we both knew and recount pre-war experiences. We talked as friends do, and it seemed incredible that we were enemies. Towards the end of the war he suffered a great deal from the Nazi régime. His daughter-in-law was imprisoned by Hitler, and he himself was removed from his command in Guernsey for daring to protest about the deportation of civilians from Guernsey and Sark.

Bob and I had practically no contacts with Occupation Forces on Sark, except for the local Commandant and doctors. The former was never allowed to call on us without some staff to spy on him, but the doctors had to talk with me privately about their patients, and often they dropped useful bits of information, sometimes, I suspected, on purpose.

As the dreary months passed slowly by, our complete isolation from the outside world weighed more and more heavily on us. All our thoughts and conversations became focused on food. We had masses of lobsters, but had no means to vary the way of cooking them, and the same was true of rabbits. When lobster is the main dish day after day, month in month out, let me assure you that you become heartily sick of the sight of it. Then we began to run out of sugar, tea, coffee and tobacco.

There was a Purchasing Commission of representatives who went over to France periodically under German escort to buy necessities for the islands. Our staunch friend, Mr. R. O. Falla, the Guernsey Chief Agricultural Officer, was chosen to serve on this commission, and he always helped our needs, especially in agriculture. By now the French themselves were also hungry and short of basic necessities, but if there was anything of the slightest use to be had Mr. Falla could be trusted to talk the French into a sale. He continued to visit us frequently.

Apparently he was impressed by the way I dealt with the Germans, and I often caught a look of amusement in his eyes as he watched me remaining seated while the officers walked up the drawing-room, bowed, kissed my hand and then bowed again when I invited them to sit down. The stiff German formality worked in my favour because it showed the Germans that I expected to be treated in my home with the rigid etiquette to which they were accustomed in their own country.

The year drew to a close with the astounding news of the Japanese raid on Pearl Harbor and the Japanese declaration of war on the U.S.A. and Great Britain. The Germans boasted to us of the sinking of the *Prince of Wales* and the *Repulse* before it was given officially by the B.B.C. News from the Far East was not encouraging. The Germans were delighted to inform us that Hong-Kong had fallen, but we had no way of knowing whether this was true. However, we did hear over our hidden wireless excerpts from Roosevelt's speech on the privilege of sacrifice. The only cheerful news that the B.B.C. could offer us for Christmas was that Mr. Churchill had arrived safely in the U.S. That was on 23 December, and the next day we got official confirmation that Hong-Kong had indeed fallen.

It was a bad ending to a bad year, and all we could do on New Year's Day was to drink a toast to 1942 in the fervent hope that it would be better than 1941.

Little did we know when we toasted the New Year that the worst hardships of German Occupation lay ahead of us. Although the routine of daily life remained the same, we had every reason to be depressed by the news, and I sometimes wondered, when I heard the nine o'clock B.B.C. broadcast, whether our hidden wireless was an asset or a liability; so many of the German boasts to which we were subjected day by day proved to be true when we listened-in a night or two later.

In spite of bad news, the shortage of food, German propaganda and the impossibility of replacing worn-out clothes, the people of Sark stubbornly refused to be downhearted and their morale remained as high as ever.

At the outbreak of war we had started a Red Cross workroom to which all my American friends subscribed most generously. With these funds we bought bales of flannel and quantities of wool. Up to the date of Occupation we had despatched three thousand garments and pairs of socks. When the Germans arrived on the island we still had a lot of material in hand which we promptly hid in various helpers' houses.

Now that our own needs had become so urgent, I used a room at the Seigneurie and started a 'Special Aid' work-room where we made eighteen hundred and seven garments for men, women and children before we ran out of material.

It was a particularly cold winter with grey skies, fierce winds blowing across the cliffs and gales which often prevented the fishing boats from putting out to sea. When the wind died down, the island was shrouded in heavy mist, and so was the sea. At last the winter ended, and Sark was bathed in sunshine and covered with every variety of spring flowers.

There was great excitement one night when a Lancaster bomber made a forced landing in a field near the Seigneurie. The plane circled round and we were awakened by the noise. Bishop, our farm bailiff, dashed up to the tower just as it came down, and at the same moment the German patrol appeared in our drive, running madly in order to take a shortcut through the field. By this time both Bob and I were up, but as the curfew was very strict no one in the house dared to go outside. We heard no shots, although Bishop said he could hear English voices. It was infuriating to be cooped up inside the house and unable to discover what was going on.

Later I got details from the German doctor who confided to me that the plane was returning from a raid on Stuttgart. The navigating instruments had been shot away and four of the crew had bailed out over France, leaving only the pilot and two others to land here. They were taken off next day to a prison in Germany, and as they went they signaled 'thumbs up' to our fishermen, the only people allowed to see them taken off from the harbour. Bob and I later persuaded the sentry who was on guard over the plane to give us some petrol for our cigarette-lighters in exchange for a bottle of very inferior kirsch from our kitchen cupboard.

By this time we were growing all our own tobacco, and matches were very scarce. We made up tobacco from vine leaves, dried clover heads, rose leaves and blackberry leaves, which we also dried and used as tea. Some of us used green pea pods for tea. Coffee was made of a mixture of barley, dried with sugar beet and parsnip, all grated or ground up together. Even home-made tobacco, disgusting though it was, helped to dull the pangs of hunger, and the craving for tobacco increased as our food stores dwindled.

Our garrison varied in numbers and we could only guess at the total. The troops commandeered all the hotels and the houses that had been left empty by the English residents when they left Sark. Miss Duckett and Miss Page, who owned the Dixcart Hotel, were still there, but the Germans were occupying a part of it.

One of the most important Germans was Freiherr von and zu Aufsess, who had been posted to Jersey early in the year and later promoted to Chief of Civil Administration. Like Prince Oettingen, he was a Bavarian and owned a wonderful old Swabian castle at Oberaufsess near Nuremberg. He was dark and broad-shouldered, a charming type of German, who had travelled widely and in peace-time had been a successful lawyer. By a curious coincidence we were in fact indirectly connected by a marriage of cousins.

One day when von Aufsess was visiting the Seigneurie, Bob remarked that in his opinion the Germans would discover before the end of the war that the Chamiel Islands would become a liability rather than an asset. This evidently registered because in 1950 when we visited von Aufsess he reminded my husband of this remark and said that at the end of the war the Germans had 30,000 troops cut off in the Channel Islands.

Both von Aufsess and Prince Oettingen, who made every effort to be fair-minded during the Occupation, were fated to suffer under the Nazi régime. Freifrau von Aufsess, who had always been a staunch anti-Nazi and refused to give the Hitler salute, was so rash as to remark after the attempted assassination of Hitler, 'What a pity they did not succeed.' This indiscretion was reported to the Gestapo, who promptly arrested her. Her fate remained unknown to her husband. When the islands were liberated von Aufsess was sent as a prisoner-of-war to England for two years, and it was only when he returned to Germany that he found that his wife had survived imprisonment by the Gestapo. In spite of this Oberaufsess remained intact. It is a fairy-tale castle which was built in the ninth century and has been in the von Aufsess family ever since. Its treasures of plate and armour are amazing, and there is a chapel with walls hung with the enamel shields of each Aufsess Baron, impaled in the arms of the family into which he married.

CHAPTER 10

TWO COMMANDO RAIDS AND
THE DEPORTATIONS

The mild subjection under which we had existed since 1940 ended in September 1942, when an order carne that all British residents in Sark, as distinct from 'island-born', were to be evacuated to Germany. Actually, only eleven people were ordered to assemble at the harbour in four days' time when they were clue to board a ship for France. A middle-aged English couple who were included in this number faced the news in a tragic state of panic. The day before they were due to leave they called at our house for a few moments and asked me to take charge of three letters and some jewellery which, they explained in a perfectly normal way, they did not wish to leave in an empty house.

Next morning I went down to the harbour with packages of sandwiches and a few little comforts which I had been able to collect for those leaving. After a long wait, Major S— and his wife did not appear and I told the Commandant that I feared something was wrong. He dashed off in one of the German cars which had been brought over to Sark for the use of officers, and after another wretched half-hour of waiting the remaining nine people to be deported were ordered on board and the boat sailed.

It was a clear morning, but the rocks off the island looked dark and grim. I stood on the quayside watching the little boat sailing away and wondered what would be the fate of its passengers. They had heard over our secret wireless sets of the unspeakable horrors in German concentration camps, and yet they had left calmly without undue fuss. After a few minutes my thoughts were jerked back to the missing couple and I hurried up the hill and along the road until I got to the house, only to find it full of Germans and entrance forbidden.

That evening all houses on the island were searched and everybody was questioned, but as no one had seen the missing couple no information was available. I had very little sleep that night and at dawn I heard a German outside the front door calling for me. When I looked out the bedroom window and asked what he wanted he told me that our friends had been found, adding would I please go to the house as soon as possible as Mrs. S— was asking for me. Within five minutes I was dressed, and with my German escort hastened to the house. Major S— was dead, and his wife was in a ghastly state, having stabbed herself in sixteen places. All I could do was to hold her hand and say soothing words. By the Grace of God she was so weak that she said nothing incriminating. Both the Commandant and the German doctor were there and did everything in their power to help; not only did they send for their own ambulance but they also ordered a boat and allowed me to telephone to the civil hospital at Guernsey and arrange for Mrs. S— to be admitted. Luckily for her, she contracted pneumonia and for many weeks was too ill to be bullied or cross-questioned.

This tragedy led to the nearest escape I had from being involved with the Gestapo. They had found a letter addressed to me in the deserted house and questioned me all one morning. They were convinced that there must be a mystery about the Major, that he was some kind of British agent. Over and over again they repeated the question, 'Have you any documents or papers?' and each time I answered that I had only the jewellery which the couple had left when they called to say good-bye. At last they left, but I felt in my bones that they intended to come back unexpectedly and search.

As the tramp of military boots died away up the drive I sat very still, thinking of a safe place to hide the letters, and after a minute or two the answer came to me. But before I hid them I had to make quite certain that no one was spying on me. Sauntering out of the front door with the letters discreetly hidden in my dress, I looked up the drive that faces the house. No signs of anyone. Then I walked to the wrought-iron gate that leads to the walled gardens and glanced up the main drive which bends left. That also was empty. A quick look at the gardens and I walked to the back of the house where we kept our chickens and rabbits. Still nobody to be seen. I hastily hit the three letters in the straw of the rabbit hutches.

My premonition was correct. In a few hours the Germans returned and the cross-examination began all over again. Suddenly the most aggressive of them produced a letter which he thrust at me, pointing to the words, 'You have our last messages.'

I took a long breath while he asked, 'What is the meaning of that?'

The word 'meaning' gave me my cue and I said firmly, 'In English, "messages" mean words spoken and not written. The messages I have are only connected with the jewellery and to whom it is to be sent if they do not return.'

My explanation was accepted and no more questions were asked, but it had been a difficult moment as up to then I had no idea that Major S— had left a letter of farewell addressed to me. I kept the hidden letters safely until after our liberation when I sent them to their addresses.

Two weeks later, British Commandos raided Sark for the first time. The raid was led by Major Geoffrey Appleyard, D.S.O., M.C. and Bar. He came with Anders Larsen, the legendary Dane who had won the V.C. and M.C. with two Bars. With them there were three other officers and five men.

Appleyard had spent several holidays in Sark and knew the island well. It was nearly midnight when the party landed on the rocks at the foot of the Hog's Back, climbed the steep cliffs and broke into a small house. In order to get in they had to smash a pane in the french window and undo the latch. The house belonged to Mrs. Pittard, whose husband had died a few months before, and so she was alone. Disturbed by the noise downstairs she came out of her bedroom thinking that the house must be on fire. She had a shock when she saw the Commandos' grotesquely blackened faces, but realised in a moment that they were English. Dressing quickly, she joined the party downstairs.

They asked about German defences and she was able to tell them where some of the guns were placed, but not what sort they were. However, she did produce a map of Sark and a copy of the *Guernsey Evening Press* with the Deportation Order. This was the first news of the deportation to reach England.

Appleyard asked if there were any German soldiers quartered nearby, and Mrs. Pittard told him that some were billeted in the annexe of the Dixcart Hotel up the valley. So the Commandos made their way along the valley to the hotel and, after killing the sentry, broke in and seized five soldiers whom they bundled outside.

The trouble began when they got into the open and the bright light of the moon showed the Germans how small the British party was. Thereupon they gave the alarm, shouting at the top of their lungs. One prisoner broke away and ran screaming towards the hotel, the others kicked and struggled madly. In spite of the fact that their arms had been trussed, three more escaped. One of these was shot and the Commandos slithered down the beach and sailed off in their boat with their one remaining prisoner.

Curiously enough, Miss Duckett and Miss Page in the main building of the Dixcart Hotel had slept through the commotion, and were only woken up at four o'clock in the morning when a German officer pushed his way into the hotel shouting, 'You have the British here.'

Every room in the hotel was ransacked and at dawn the Gestapo arrived. As Miss Duckett and Miss Page had heard nothing and seen nothing, they found it quite impossible to extract any information from them.

At nine o'clock that morning a German arrived at the Seigneurie and informed me that the Commandant had given an order that the junior school and every small house and cottage in the centre of the island were to be taken over by the troops, and evacuation completed by midday. The owners moved out with all possible speed to their friends and relations, taking as many of their belongings as they were able to cart with them.

I hurried to the school where I was met by Philip Le Feuvre, the carter, with my two-horse van. We were working hard to shift school desks and books when a message came from the Commandant ordering the van to go at once to the Dixcart Hotel. I said to Philip Le Feuvre, 'Go down on foot and tell the Commandant that if my van is taken we cannot possibly evacuate the school furniture and books by midday.'

The Commandant sent back a message to say that it would be all right if the school was cleared later on in the day, but the van must go at once to the hotel. So off it went, and we were left to move the paraphernalia out into the road. When the van eventually appeared, I asked Philip Le Feuvre what had happened, and he told me that he had been ordered to take two coffins to the harbour. By this time we all knew that there had been a raid but not what the outcome of it had been. 'Do you think the dead men were English?' I asked.

'No, I think they must have been Germans because there were swastikas on the coffins and they were draped with German flags.'

Two days later the German propagandists condemned the illegal tying of prisoners' hands, and during a powerful speech in Edinburgh the following week Mr. Churchill announced that the Germans had shackled the hands of all British prisoners. He was referring to the 1,376 prisoners taken at the Dieppe landing, in which the Canadians took part. The chaining of 1,376 German prisoners in Canada was promptly ordered in reply. So altogether 2,752 prisoners were manacled as a direct result of the first Commando raid on our tiny island. It seemed a heavy price to pay for the capture of one prisoner and a copy of the *Guernsey Evening Press*.

It was some time before the Germans noticed the missing pane in Mrs. Pittard's house but she was soon forced to tell the whole story of the Commandos' visit. As soon as she broke down under the relentless questions, she was put into a van, taken to the harbour, shipped to Guernsey and imprisoned there. Perhaps the Germans found it in their hearts to sympathise with a lone widow still in mourning for her husband, for they treated her with courtesy and after several weeks, without any reason given, she was released and allowed to return home.

Following this raid, life in Sark became much harder for us. More barbed wire than ever was put up and over 13,000 landmines were laid on the land at the top of the cliffs. In many cases the mines were placed on some of our best agricultural land. The rabbits bred in the mine-fields, coming out at night to eat all our crops. The Germans stole all our snares during the hours of curfew so that we could not catch any of the rabbits ourselves. Another result of the raid was that the German Commandant in Sark was replaced and all troops were moved to the centre of the island.

Now no paths were open to the sea except at the harbour, and we had to get a permit to go there in order to collect sea water to cook with, as our salt had run out. It is impossible to describe the taste of bread made with dehydrated salt water. Not only were we now entirely without tea, coffee and tobacco, but we were also out of soap, and the men's clothes were getting beyond repair. It was a common sight to see men wearing jackets made of old tablecloths and curtains, or darned with wools of every conceivable colour. There were no new shoes for the children and the only way of dealing with this problem was to cut the toes of their shoes as their feet grew.

Every week the Commandant brought me numerous notices which he wished me to sign and put on view and enforce, but I steadfastly refused to sign anything and my answer was always the same, 'These are German orders and not mine, so you can sign them and affix the Wehrmacht stamp. Then I will see that they are obeyed.' The orders were mostly concerned with requisitions, demolitions or

146

boats. One day the Commandant arrived with a notice, which read
as follows:

THE CONTROLLING COMMITTEE OF THE
STATES OF GUERNSEY
IMPORTANT NOTICE

Issued by Order of the German Authorities

'Sexual relations, either with German soldiers or with civilians,
are strictly forbidden during the next three months. In cases of non-
compliance with this Order, severe punishment by the Occupying
Authorities is to be expected, even if no infection takes place.'

(signed) DR. DESCHAUER,
Standortsarzt

(signed) A. N. SYMONS,
Health Services Officer

20 October 1942.

The limit had been reached and as far as this notice was concerned I intended to go on strike. Looking the Commandant
squarely in the face with no attempt to hide my disgust, I said, 'This
has nothing whatsoever to do with Sark. We are in no way under
control from the States of Guernsey, and I will not publish anything
so insulting to my people.'

Later, when Bob and I were alone in my study, I said, 'This is the
latest *billet doux* from the Commandant, handed to me when he
called today. As usual he wanted me to sign it, have it put on view
and enforce it. Now what do you think of that?'

Bob grinned, 'I think it's a highly indecent communication for a
German officer to present to a lady. Tell me — did he look embarrassed when he handed it to you?'

'He looked embarrassed by the time I had given him a piece of
my mind.'

'I bet he did. By the way, did you ask him why they have set a time-limit of three months? The German mind is so methodical that there must be some very good reason for it.'

'No, I didn't. I was too angry.'

'They must be having a lot of fun and games in Guernsey, which is more than can be said of Sark.'

That was true enough. As a matter of fact there was only one illegitimate child born of a German father in Sark throughout the five years of Occupation. It must be admitted that some of our farmers indulged in black market activities and sold their butter to the Germans for as much as ten marks a pound, a dastardly thing to do when butter was desperately short. The few who were guilty of collaboration with the Germans aroused great bitterness among the majority.

I knew for certain that we had one Quisling on the island, because the German Commandant told me that she had helped to select the people she most disliked for deportation. How any woman could take revenge on her neighbours in this way is beyond my comprehension, but one can only assume that she had no knowledge of conditions in German concentration camps and prisons. Another rather eccentric English woman was very pro-German and used to say 'Heil Hitler' when employed by the Germans to act as interpreter in their office. Her sentiments led to an amusing incident in one of the shops where she was holding forth in the presence of the vicar's wife about the damage done to Cologne Cathedral, ending up dramatically with, 'What would Christ have said had He been on earth?' To which the vicar's lady retorted, 'At least He would not have said "Heil Hitler".'

I am afraid that this brisk repartee was reported to the Germans and was the real cause of the vicar and his wife being deported the following year, in spite of all I could do to prevent it by arguing and pleading that there could be no marriages, or baptisms, or burials without a vicar. Had the pro-German woman seen Coventry

The Royal Standard flying on the Seigneurie during the Queen's visit

With her Majesty the Queen and the duke of Edinburgh

Cathedral, which had been completely gutted several months previously by German bombers, or the Auschwitz concentration camp, she might well have asked herself what Christ would have said had He been on earth. But no one on Sark knew about these things until after the war.

Looking about me that grey winter of 1942 I felt that in many ways we could count ourselves lucky. True we were caged in by miles of barbed wire and thousands of land-mines, and we were very hungry and short of most necessities; but we had survived two and a half years of Occupation without showing any signs of defeatism. Apart from the tragedy of Major S— and his wife and the nine other English who had been deported, all Sark families had been able to remain on the island.

My husband's companionship at this time gave me great confidence. Officially, he kept aloof from the business of running the island and ensuring that orders were enforced, but his sense of humour and his advice heartened me. In spite of hunger, hardship and the fight to preserve such rights as were possible for the people of Sark, I had not so far suffered loneliness. Bob and I worked together. There was no problem that I could not discuss with him, and one of them was the cost of the Occupation which was straining the finances of the island. The Germans had said that they would pay two-thirds, but of course they never did and, even if they had done, it would have been in their specially printed Occupation marks which they still valued at two shillings and one penny and which we knew had no real value.

In spite of all the work and worry we occasionally found time to make up a game of bridge with our friends before the evening curfew. By now every pack of cards on the island was in a disgracefully shabby condition and there were no score cards, but while playing we could make believe that life had returned to normal. After dinner — such as it was — we listened to the nine o'clock news in the boxroom, and then Bob and I went downstairs to my study to discuss the news and speculate on what was happening in England and America.

We were able to send and receive messages through the Red Cross, but they were so censored that my only way of letting my family know how hungry we were was confined to allusions to Mrs. Beeton. Many Red Cross messages failed to reach us, but Amice, my eldest daughter, managed to let me know that she had contacted one of the men who had taken part in the Commando raid by mentioning that she had news of Sophie Moffatt's daughter from a recent visitor. As Sophie Moffatt was my mother's maiden name it was clear that at last my family had uncensored news of Sark.

The news of our first victory reached Sark on 5 November 1942. We could hardly believe our ears when we turned on the wireless and heard of General Alexander's special communiqué to the effect that the 8th Army had broken right through the German defences at El Alamein, taken nine thousand troops, killed Rommel's Chief of Staff and captured the next senior officer. I heard after the war from one of my English friends that the B.B.C. had broken into a programme after the nine o'clock broadcast on 4 November, and that the announcer's voice had shaken with excitement as he read the statement.

Since 1940 we had become accustomed to defeat and retreats. Our troops had been cleared out of France, Belgium, Holland, Norway, Crete and Greece. Germany occupied all Europe and a large sector of Russian territory as well. There had been advances and retreats through North Africa, the last retreat culminating in the fall of Tobruk. Now at long last it seemed to us that the tide of war was turning. But as the German official news agency merely stated, 'The High Command reports today that the German-Italian tank corps has withdrawn to the second-line prepared defence positions in several sectors. This does not mean a decision in the enemy's favour,' it would have been foolhardy to announce that we knew better, because the only way we could have known the truth was through our secret radio sets.

The Channel Islanders were again to be severely punished for the Commando raid on Sark, and more deportations were ordered from the islands in February 1943. Orders came for some sixty-three people to be taken from Sark, their ages ranging from eight to seventy. My husband was among them. I was told that all men who had held a commission were now to be sent to prisoner-of-war camps in Germany and it had been discovered that Bob had been an officer in the Royal Flying Corps during the First World War. We could not understand what advantage it could be to the Germans to take children and women of all ages; however, I was informed that the order came from the 'Highest Command'.

The scene could scarcely have been more dismal when we gathered at the harbour. A bitter wind was blowing in from the sea which was looking particularly sinister, and rain pelted down viciously from a leaden sky. By far the most pathetic figure on the quayside was Mrs. Pittard, who had not yet recovered from the shock of her imprisonment in Guernsey and was now about to face an unknown fate in Germany. Miss Duckett and Miss Page were also there. Although we were all cold and wet and miserable, those who were about to leave and those who remained tried to reassure one another. All round me I could hear men and women saying the same things.

'Take care of yourself.'

'Don't worry about me. I'll be all right.'

'Let me know how you get on.'

'The war can't go on forever.'

'Of course it can't. I shall probably be home again soon.'

I made an effort to comfort the mothers by saying, 'Try not to worry too much about the children. You know the soldiers have been very kind to them here. I spent a long time working in Germany after the last war and noticed then how fond the Germans were of children.'

It was almost a relief when the party was ordered on board and the boat cast off, turned in the harbour, edged its way through the narrow entrance and headed towards the grey seas outside the harbour. We stood on the quayside, waving to the people on deck; then, as the boat disappeared, we turned back and the forlorn procession made its way through the rock tunnel and up the steep hill, past the Germans guarding the harbour. There was no sign of gloating, it was almost as if they sympathized with us. Having climbed the hill we made our separate ways home. Little did we know that it would be two and a half years before we could welcome our friends and relations home again.

The deportees from Sark joined those from Guernsey, as we learnt later, and they were all packed into stinking boats and filthy trains. The women and children were herded into makeshift quarters in the grandstand of a race-course near Paris where the conditions were lamentable, and then transferred to Biberach. Although food and accommodation were very poor the children were well cared for by a German Red Cross sister. That was the only comfort.

My husband was taken with other men to Laufen, an old Schloss built for the Bishops of Salzburg in the Middle Ages, where the living quarters were overcrowded and the walls full of bugs. With typical Yankee cussedness, Bob announced his refusal to set foot on German soil unless he was forced to do so. He could not avoid the daily parade, but he sometimes appeared smoking a pipe and when the parade was called to attention he promptly stood at ease. One day the German sergeant said, 'I want to ask a favour of you. Would you mind not smoking on parade?' Bob replied, 'Now you've asked me that way, I won't do it again.'

At the end he was excused parades on the ground of ill health.

I was able to write open letters to him through the German post and he was able to send letters to England, so I actually got more news of my family in England through him then I did in Sark.

There was nothing of any use that I could send him except onions, which were welcome because they gave flavour to the interminable, tasteless soup. All that was left in the way of drinks at the Seigneurie now was one bottle of whisky and one of brandy which were kept strictly for emergencies; but when it seemed to me that Bob was in dire need of home cheer, I decided to send a little of both. I filled a medicine bottle with whisky, labelled it 'Eyewash' and hid it in a case of onions. It got through safely so I followed it up with a little brandy labelled 'Sleeping Draught'.

Two months after the deportations in February the islands were again in trouble. Allied planes had attacked German ships plying between Granville and the islands. There was a joint Purchasing Commission in Granville and the ships, several of which had been sunk, had been bound for Jersey and Guernsey carrying food for the islands. Reprisal followed swiftly – rations were cut and on 30 April a notice appeared in the official island newspapers:

'The British Military Command, disregarding the fact that the population of the Channel Islands are their OWN COUNTRYMEN, are attempting in every way to jeopardize the continuous supply to the Islands by incessant NUISANCE RAIDS. If in consequence of these raids the RATIONS of the ISLAND POPULATION have now to be decreased, the population can thank for this their countrymen ON THE OTHER SIDE OF THE CHANNEL. Churchill and his supporters will not achieve any military success from such nuisance raids. But it characterises their notorious lack of scruples that they do not refrain from exposing their own fellow countrymen to suffering that could be avoided. THE POPULATION OF THE ISLANDS, HOWEVER, MAY AT LEAST KNOW THE CUL PRITS.'

We knew full well that the severe cuts in our rations were not really due to any shortage caused by shipping losses, but were merely a gratuitous revenge. The islanders could not be held responsible for legitimate acts of war by the Allies. As for 'lack of scruples', it seemed to us that scruples had been conspicuous by their absence during the recent deportations of old women and young children to concentration camps in Germany. Now our bread ration was reduced from four pounds a week to three, and meat to two ounces a fortnight. Naturally I protested to the local Commandant. 'How do you expect our men to work on empty stomachs? Civilian rations are already dangerously low. Your troops commandeer most of the fish and crops and farm products, leaving a minimum for civilian consumption. If these new cuts are enforced you will suffer much more than we will because our fishermen and farmers won't have the necessary physical ability to meet your demands, and that will be your fault, not ours.'

He shrugged his shoulders and said tiredly, 'I'm sorry – very sorry — but it's an order.'

Actually I was not particularly worried about the fishermen and farmers. I reckoned they would make out all right, come what might. I was much more concerned about the children. Fortunately we still had half a pint of full milk per head every day from our own beautiful Guernsey cows, although Guernsey was limited to skim milk four days a week. As we had no cooking fats I protested to the local Commandant every time the Germans attempted to seize more milk. Needless to say, our farmers took good care to skim the milk for the troops, and when I received a complaint that the Germans were finding it impossible to make enough butter from the milk, I announced that I would go myself to watch them churn it. They were aghast when I arrived dressed in a white overall and, armed with a large thermometer, proceeded to give a long lecture on butter making which got them so confused that I never had another complaint.

Although the children remained remarkably healthy, those who were getting their second teeth during the Occupation were unfortunate because the diet was short of calcium. Also the lack of soap encouraged lice and I regularly visited the school with a pair of knitting needles which I used to part the children's hair in a search for 'foreign bodies'. In spite of every possible precaution most of the children suffered at some time or another from impetigo, which I have since been told was also prevalent in England.

One of the most tiresome problems I had to sort out concerned the electric light supply. The Germans had made us take three engines from private houses and link them together to supply electricity for their own use. These engines were continually breaking down and I finally wrote a very angry letter to the Commandant in Guernsey protesting about the cost to the island. Major-General Muller, a bombastic gentleman who would have made a perfect music-hall character, did not come to face me himself, but sent one of his underlings, a rough, uncouth officer from East Prussia, whose name was Zachau. This man had the impertinence to shout at me, 'This is not the way to write to the Commandant.'

I put on a completely blank expression and said, 'If you shout I shall not understand a word of what you are saying. In England we never shout when we talk business.'

Zachau was so taken aback that his jaw dropped and he positively gaped at me. It was a satisfaction to put him in his right place. He returned to Guernsey and I heard no more about breakdowns in the electric supply.

By now the islanders had no artificial light of any kind and during the winter months, when daylight faded early in the evening, they had nothing to do but go to bed at sundown or sit by their firelight in the gloom. Even firelight was a luxury because of the scarcity of wood. Gorse, which flourished along the coastline and could have been used for fuel, was cut off from us by miles of barbed wire entanglements.

The troops solved their fuel problems quite simply by tearing down the empty wooden bungalows which had been vacated in 1940 by British residents. All wooden furniture found in the bungalows was chopped up and burnt.

But in spite of privations, restrictions, the shortage of food and all the nonsense of Occupation, the people of Sark absolutely refused to show any signs of alarm or despondency. Sometimes the Germans commented on this obvious self-confidence to me and each time I would say smugly, 'There is no reason why we should be depressed. We know that the Allies will win in the end and even if the day of victory is a long way ahead there is no doubt in our minds about the outcome.'

Life at the Seigneurie was lonely for me without Bob, but I was still in possession of my house, my cattle and even my two dogs who lived mostly on fish offal and potatoes. It was a nerve-racking wait but I knew that the end was sure.

When the war began to go badly for the Germans on the Russian front they seemed to harbour grave doubts about their own victory. The soldiers no longer sang as they marched along the roads and I got an impression that they were secretly frightened and wondering what their position would be if they not only lost the war but were also held responsible for any ill- treatment of us. Their officers still maintained a show of invincibility although they must have guessed that we were getting news of heavy bombing of German towns, reversals on the Russian front and our victory in North Africa.

There was an underground news service known as G.U.N.S., which stood for Guernsey Underground News Service. This was started by Charles Machon, a linotype operator on the Guernsey *Star*, and was the biggest of several secret news sheets in the islands.

Three copies on thin, tightly folded paper were smuggled into Sark regularly, at great risk to the men who carried them tucked behind a hat-band or hidden in the heel of a shoe. G.U.N.S. was delivered to two men in Sark — one of these being Mr. Wakley, the carrier, and the other Mr. Hubert Lanyon, the baker and general storekeeper.

It was not until March 1944 that the Germans found out who was running G.U.N.S. Charles Machon was taken to prison, 'grilled' by the Gestapo and later died in hospital. The men who had worked with him were deported. Mr. Lanyon also suffered when it was discovered that he had been receiving copies. The Germans tried un-successfully to make him admit who else saw it, and on one occasion even went so far as to knock him unconscious. He was sentenced to six months' imprisonment, but only served four and so escaped being sent to the Continent.

Although the fortunes of war had favoured us in 1943, the year ended with grim reminders of the price being paid by those fighting for their country. Towards the end of October' the British cruiser *Charybdis* was sunk by German torpedo boats in the Channel. Three weeks later the bodies of some nineteen ratings were washed ashore at Jersey, Guernsey and Sark, and became the gruesome items in an official report on recovery of corpses from the Island Police to the President of the Controlling Committee.

On this occasion the Germans showed the respect which is held by all good fighting forces towards a gallant enemy. A mass funeral with full military honours was arranged, the islanders were allowed to show their loyalty and express thanks to the men fighting for their freedom, and the response was overwhelming. There were more than seven hundred wreaths and no censorship on the inscriptions, 'They died that we might be free.'

I doubt if Major-General Muller would have shown such chiv-alry, but a few weeks previously he had been sent to a command on the Eastern front and his place had been taken by Count von Schmettow, who had now moved his headquarters from Jersey to Guernsey.

For us Christmas was marred by the second Commando raid on Sark, led by Lieutenant McGonigal. The first landing proved a fail-ure and the party eventually followed Appleyard's route and reached the top of the Hog's Back where disaster overtook them. There were violent explosions which wounded two men. The others tried des-perately to drag them clear, but it was soon obvious that the party had come right through a mine-field. More mines exploded as they tried to make their way back down the steep cliff to the waiting boat, and the wounded men were killed. All but one of the remaining party were wounded, but somehow they managed to reach the boat.

Alerted by the explosions the Germans sent patrols out to investigate, but nothing was discovered until daybreak when the two mangled corpses with blackened faces were found. There were also trails of blood leading back to the sea.

Although the Commandos had failed on this occasion, from then on the Occupying forces were kept in suspense. When there was no moonlight and the island was shrouded in eerie darkness, German troops were uneasy and on the alert. So in a strange way even this raid helped to undermine German morale. It also reminded us that we had not been forgotten or entirely forsaken.

The only women friends who came to stay with me during the Occupation were Countess Blücher, her sister, Ella Radziwill, and Olive de Sausmarez. They all three lived in Guernsey and, of course, had to get special German permits to cross to Sark. Except for these three I never had any house guests to whom I could talk freely. The position of Countess Blücher was difficult vis-à-vis the Germans, as she was the widow of Lothair Blücher, who was a British subject, her son had served in the British Army and been killed fighting in Tunisia, and she and her sister were both Russian-born. Not only was it a joy to me to have them under my roof, but we sometimes managed to get a fourth for a game of bridge.

CHAPTER 11

LIBERATION

It was a fine sunny morning in the early summer of 1944. I had just finished my breakfast of fried mashed potatoes and a cup of the noxious brew which passed as coffee when the German doctor appeared. Closing the door of my study and looking very mysterious, with a finger to his lips, he said in a low tone of voice, as if he were frightened of being overheard. 'You must tell nobody or I will be shot, but I have news for you. The Allies have landed on the French coast between Cherbourg and Le Havre.' He added hurriedly, 'Of course it is probably only another raid like the one at Dieppe, but I will come back when I can and tell you what is happening.'

Before I could even say 'Thank you' he had disappeared. Now I suddenly remembered that during the night I had been half awakened twice by the sound of heavy bombers droning overhead. I dashed out to find Bishop and his wife, and for the first time in daylight we rushed to our hidden radio and heard one of the broadcasts from the B.B.C.

This was 6 June 1944, D-Day. The Second Front had started. We heard the announcement that the King would broadcast at nine o'clock that evening and that the Lord Mayor of Melbourne in his broadcast had quoted the famous prayer of Lord Astley before the Battle of Edgehill:

'Lord, Thou knowest that I shall be verie busie this day.
I may forget Thee. But do not Thou forget me.'

It was an almost unbearable strain to pretend that we knew nothing and to avoid showing the slightest sign of excitement. By now dozens of tiny crystal sets had been made up from instructions given out by the B.B.C., and almost every house had one hidden some-where.

Day by day we heard the thunder of guns and at night we watched the flashes and lights which gave us a clue to the Allies' advance along the coast of France opposite and plainly visible to us.

By 9 June we knew that General Alexander was fifty miles past Rome and was talking about the 'catastrophe' suffered by the 14th German Army. But the weather, which was grey with gusty winds and rain, was not favouring us in France. Although we seemed to be doing as well as could be expected, we began to realise that there was still a great deal of hard fighting ahead. Then we got the news that London was being attacked by flying-bombs.

The Germans gloatingly claimed that London was a sea of flames, that the Government had evacuated to the North, that the trains were crowded with terror-stricken Cockneys. We had no way of knowing how much of this was true. People of Sark who had refused to evacuate still had their families with them, but the people of Guernsey and Jersey, many of whom had sent their children and old people to England, must have suffered agonies of doubt and fear. I, too, was very worried. Apart from my family I had many friends in England and could only guess their exact whereabouts. If a member of my immediate family were killed, presumably the news would eventually reach me, but I would remain ignorant about the fate of my friends. To make matters worse, we were no longer receiving regular Red Cross messages, and our only information was gleaned from the B.B.C. bulletins which were, of course, strictly censored.

Three weeks went by, and at long last, on 2 July it was announced that we had taken 43,000 prisoners at Cherbourg, and that enemy resistance had virtually ended there. If the Germans were to be believed, flying-bombs were raining down by day and night on London and the casualties were horrific. Since D-Day the islands had been without any imports of food or essential supplies from France. Mr. Churchill had always insisted on the principle that the Germans were solely responsible for the food supplies of the countries they had occupied, and soon after D-Day he urged upon the Admiralty more strenuous efforts to see that no Germans escaped out of the Channel Islands and that no food supplies got in. This instruction had been vigorously enforced. On 18 September a directive about the Channel Islands, signed by General Keitel, was issued from Supreme Headquarters in Berlin. Civilian rations, it said, had to be reduced to the 'barest survival level'. If supplies of food were still insufficient then the entire civil population, except for able-bodied men, had to be 'pushed over to the enemy. The directive ended, 'An order will follow for the complete stoppage of rations for the civilian population and for measures to inform the British Government that this has been done.'

The next day there was a directive from Hitler himself, which announced that an approach should be made through a neutral power to Britain and America. If they would not supply the civilians, everybody except able-bodied men would be removed from the islands. The Commander-in-Chief in the West was ordered to discuss evacuation plans with the Navy. What was to happen to the evacuees was not explained, and apparently Hitler did not care.

Count von Schmettow reported that about seventy to seventy-five percent of the civilians were working for the Germans either directly, or indirectly and even if the remainder were removed the garrison would achieve no more than an extra month's supplies of food. Supreme Headquarters in Berlin paid no heed to this information and no action of any kind was taken by either side.

In September our Harvest Festival was celebrated in the time-honoured way, but there were only token decorations in the Church. The precious gifts of soap, bread, tobacco leaves, butter and eggs which had been laid around the pulpit and the communion table the previous year were absent. Prices paid at the auction which followed the Festival give an indication of the living conditions in Sark at that time. No food of any description was put up for auction, only flavourings were offered. A large bottle of Flag sauce, which in pre-war days cost about a shilling, was knocked down for £5.10.0, tax not included. Half an ounce of cloves and one or two packets of Chivers lemon crystals went for 6/- each. A sixpenny tin of Vim fetched 14/- . Single boxes of matches were bought for prices ranging between 21/- and 33/-. A baby's bottle-teat and end was sold for £3.1.0 and this without the bottle. As rubber teats and ends were irreplaceable, these commodities commanded an exorbitant price, even though they were second- or third-hand. Women who have been half-starved during pregnancy are not likely to produce adequate milk for their babies, and so baby bottles were of paramount importance, both in Guernsey and Sark.

One morning a few days after the auction sale the German doctor arrived as usual to tell me about the islanders who were under his care. He seemed to have something on his mind, but I was at a loss to know what it was until he remarked: 'I hear Guernsey has been warned that it may be necessary to draw indiscriminately on flour and potatoes. They say that all the stored grain and ninety percent of the potato crop would in that case be commandeered.' There was a slight pause and then he concluded, 'I know you have many affairs to attend to, so I will not take up any more of your time.'

Time — that was the operative word. It was clear that we must work quickly to circumvent this danger. All the wheat grown in the island had to be taken to the Village Hall and stored under German orders, but the Germans had never thought of placing a guard there, so we had a sporting chance of raiding it. I consulted Bishop, my farm manager, and he contacted Mr. Baker (now our Seneschal) and Philip Le Feuvre, the carter. They knew that if we were caught the consequences would be extremely serious, but my loyal helpers did not even pause to consider that side of the problem.

Zero hour was 6 p.m., when we knew the Germans had their evening meal. We had to take into account the sentry who was posted on the top of the old mill and could see the road. Fortunately the Hall itself was screened by trees and even if the sentry saw a cart on the road near-by his suspicion was not likely to be aroused before the curfew. Nevertheless, if he was on the alert he might notice that the cart remained out of sight for an unusual length of time, and investigate.

The cart, with some empty sacks, arrived at the Hall and while I kept watch outside the three men went inside and in an incredibly short space of time filled all the sacks. Then the cart jogged on down the road, turned into my drive and we unloaded our booty at the small mill inside my barn. We had managed to get away with nearly a ton of wheat. We ground and portioned it out into small bags which Mr. Lanyon, our baker, secretly distributed to the people with their bread rations.

Our next consideration was the problem of the potato crop. If the Germans commandeered ninety percent, the civil population would be faced with starvation — no protests or pleading on my part would have the slightest effect. But I had one asset which they knew nothing about. It so happens that there is a trap-door in the floor of my drawing-room, with plenty of storage space below. The floor is covered by a very large carpet, and a sofa sits directly over the trap-door. Our scheme was quite simple. People brought as many potatoes as they dared save from the Germans, and these were hidden under the drawing-room floor and doled out when necessary.

But in spite of the precautions we had taken, hunger stalked the island. The situation became so desperate that during the first week of November the Bailiff of Guernsey was allowed to contact the International Red Cross over the radio transmitter. His message read:

To the Secretary-General,   Guernsey,
International Red Cross,   5th November, 1944
Geneva

Conditions rapidly deteriorating here. Will soon become impossible. . . . we urge immediate visit of Red Cross representative.

All rations drastically reduced.
Bread finishes 15th December.
Sugar finishes 6th January.

Ration of separated milk will be reduced to one third pint per head by end of year.

Soap and other cleansers — stocks completely exhausted.

Vegetables generally inadequate to supply civilian population through winter. German consumption heavy . . .

Clothing and footwear stocks almost exhausted.

Gas and electricity finish at the end of year.

Coal stocks exhausted. Wood fuel quite inadequate.

Many essential medical supplies already finished.

VICTOR G. CAREY,
Bailiff of Guernsey.

Anaesthetics were in such short supply that they could only be used for urgent operations, and many essential drugs were exhausted. There was no soap except for hospital use in Guernsey and even that was inadequate. As Sark was supplied by Guernsey the Bailiff's report was also of vital concern to us. There was much talk of supplies from the Red Cross, and we waited hopefully for a ship to bring the food to save us, but as the days and weeks passed our hopes faded.

By now everyone on the island, including the troops, had a lean and hungry look. We had become gradually acclimatized to hunger, but the Germans, who are notoriously heavy eaters, and who up to now had lived on the fat of the land, were quite incapable of adapting themselves to a near-starvation diet and began prowling around at night stealing everything they could lay hands on. They stole our chickens, calves and pigs, even cats and dogs to supplement their rations. The stealing became such a serious nuisance that I told the local German Commandant, 'You haven't got an army. You've only got a pack of thieves and beggars.'

I was much too occupied during the day to be aware of hunger, but each night in bed I was conscious of a strange feeling that my stomach was touching my spine. Although I kept up the habit of eating in the dining-room during the summer months, this was impossible during the winter because of the shortage of fuel, and so I had my food, such as it was, brought in on a tray to my sitting-room.

I had by now read every book in the house; the most satisfactory, because the longest, was *Gone With the Wind*. How I sympathized with Scarlett O'Hara when the South was near starvation at the end of the Civil War. The description of her waking up in the morning and imagining that she smelt bacon being fried in the kitchen and the aroma of freshly-made coffee came home to me with special force.

When there was nothing more to read I amused myself by thinking of all the cruises I had taken. In my mind I would go over my trip to India, recalling the people I had met on board; the bridge games, the backgammon and the Mah-Jong with the Maharajahs and members of their suites; the fantastic speed and memory of the Indians — how they had turned each Mah-Jong piece down and re-membered exactly where it was; the ports we had put into, and the unloading and loading of the cargoes; my astonishment at seeing a red-headed negro. It was a perfect form of escapism.

Every Saturday night I went to bed thanking God that we had survived one more week, in spite of the fact that, as always during the winter, there were many days when the fishermen could not put out to sea and no fish arrived on the island. There was nothing merry about that Christmas of 1944 and we had no cause for rejoicing. The Christmas carols we heard over the B.B.C., far from heartening us, brought back nostalgic memories of pre-war Christmases of peace and plenty. I wondered how Bob was faring in Laufen that day, and whether Amice had managed to find a Christmas tree and presents for her children, and whether Jehanne was with her.

Although it had been a dismal Christmas, the New Year was made wonderfully happy by the arrival of the old Swedish ship *Vega*, chartered by the Red Cross. Sufficient parcels were brought in every fortnight for each person to have one. They contained ¼lb. sugar, ½lb. butter, tea, raisins, prunes, corned beef, Spam, chocolate, tinned milk, cheese, biscuits and salt, but no flour. Nothing had ever tasted so marvellous as our first Spam.

Directly the parcels began to arrive the Germans cut down all our rations. They took sixty percent of our fish and gave us forty, reserving the best of the catch for themselves, and announced that they would take all our seed potatoes, ninety-two percent of the others, and cattle. But it was becoming increasingly clear to us and to them that the end of the war was not far off. The troops were seen feverishly dragging guns to new places. Anti-glider posts made of iron girders and railway lines were put up in the fields, ruining our spring crops. The iron girders had small bombs on them and were called 'Rommel's Asparagus' by the soldiers.

Count von Schmettow, who had been Commander-in-Chief of the Channel Islands since 1940, was replaced by Admiral Huffmeier in February 1945. The reason for this was that he had fallen out of favour with Hitler, who had begun to mistrust the German Army after the July plot on his life and was putting his faith in the Navy.

Huffmeier was a tall, burly, fanatic Nazi, who modelled himself on Hitler as an orator. The official excuse given for von Schmettow's recall to Germany was 'reasons of health', and he himself told us after the war that he had been summoned to Admiral Crancke, who accused him of being soft in his treatment of the islands and deficient in zeal. He fully expected to be 'liquidated' but he was saved by his uncle, General von Rundstedt.

After Huffmeier arrived, it was astonishing to see how the morale of the Germans varied from day to day. Sometimes we could hear them being ordered to sing, which they did unwillingly, while they worked. Then, a few days later, when they heard news of the V-2 rockets which were falling on London, their spirits soared. Nearly every day they were given 'pep talks' by their officers, and Huffmeier made it his business to come over from Guernsey and address the troops vehemently. He told them that they were to fight to the end and to be the last Germans to surrender, and it so happened that they *were*.

On 1 May we heard on the nine o'clock news the terse statement, 'Hitler is dead.' Five days later, the troops had become so disaffected that Huffmeier only dared address them in an open field, after their arms had been piled on one side. He told them that they would be brutally treated if they were taken prisoner.

We all knew that it was now only a question of hours before the total surrender of Germany, but the people of Sark had to control their excitement because we were still under military occupation. On 7 May we got an order to deliver cattle the next day and a requisition for two hundred tons of timber trees to be cut for the Germans. But we did not bother to obey because we heard the next morning that Admiral Doenitz had surrendered and by eleven o'clock I had the Union jack and the Stars and Stripes flying from my tower.

A gathering of the inhabitants was quickly arranged by verbal messages, and all assembled at the island Hall at 3 p.m. to hear Mr. Churchill on the radio. When Mr. Churchill referred to 'our dear Channel Islands' , saying that they were now free, we looked at each other and smiled because we still had 275 Germans all around us.

As far as we could tell the German troops had gone to ground; neither hair nor hide of them was seen, and we paid no attention to the curfew. Late that night we had a huge bonfire blazing on the cliffs, material for which had been quietly and secretly collected for some days beforehand. We heard afterwards from the Navy that our bonfire was the only one in the Channel Islands. It had been sighted from a distance north of Alderney the night before the actual surrender, and the Navy had feared that it was Germans carrying out sabotage.

Next day we could see H.M.S. *Beagle* lying at anchor off Guernsey harbour with other ships, and a number of planes circled over us, dropping coloured flares. We waited in a fever of excitement for the arrival of the British, but no boat from Guernsey was sighted for two days and we felt terribly let down. The explanation was quite simple. The British force had not landed on Guernsey till 9 May and the Occupation troops on Sark had refused to answer telephone calls from Guernsey. This ostrich-like behaviour gave rise to a rumour that there must be 'trouble in Sark'. So at about five o'clock in the evening on 10 May a tug came over with only three officers and twenty men, and I went to the harbour to meet our 'Liberation Force'. Not a German was to be seen anywhere. Colonel Allen, the English officer in charge of the party, asked where they were and added that he would need an interpreter. I informed him that I would act as interpreter and led him to the house that the Germans used as their *Kommandantur*. But no Germans were about and it was only after one of our soldiers hammered loudly on the door that they appeared and the German major who was in charge was summoned to answer Colonel Allen's questions. When he had done so satisfactorily Colonel Allen turned to me. 'I can't leave any troops here because so far only a token force has been landed in Guernsey.' He hesitated a moment and then asked, 'Would you mind being left for a few days, or would you prefer to return to Guernsey with me?'

There was a glint in his eyes when I said tartly, 'As I have been left for nearly five years I can stand a few more days."

'That's fine. Now will you tell the German Commandant that he is to carry out whatever orders you give until our troops come over?'

Having translated this command, I promptly gave my first order to the German major: 'You will see to it that the telephone is laid on at once to my house and kept open day and night so that I can contact Guernsey.'

Our Liberation Force boarded the tug and I was left in command of 275 German troops! Next day I gave three orders. First, to remove mines from the harbour; second, to remove the anti-glider posts from among our crops; and third, to hand back our wireless sets.

It gave me enormous satisfaction after all these years to be giving orders over the telephone to the Germans and saying, 'Repeat, please,' and then to hear the German voice answer, *'Zu, Befehl, Gnädige Frau.'*

The fishermen told me that the roll-bombs hanging over our harbour were held by such rusty wire that they might crash down when our troops arrived, so I gave an order that they were to be removed, and was slightly taken aback when the Commandant telephoned to say that two of his soldiers had been killed while obeying this order. The only reply I could think of at that moment was, '*Ach, so?*' There was a pause and then he asked if the soldiers could be buried in our cemetery.

'Yes, but our grave-diggers are to make their graves.'

Another long pause and then the tentative voice enquired, 'Would it be permitted to fire a volley over their graves?'

This request came as a complete surprise and I felt that it was not for me to give permission, so I telephoned Brigadier Snow, who was in command of the Liberation Forces in Guernsey, and he gave his consent.

Next day a launch was sent to take me to dine in H.M.S. *Beagle*. I shall never forget that meal. No feast of Lucullus could have compared with it. Before we sat down to dine Captain Williams asked me What I had missed most during the Occupation, and I said, 'Hot baths and the smell of frying bacon.' He promptly ordered a special savoury bacon to be cooked for me, but by the time it was put before me I was conscious of a lump in my throat and was quite unable to do more than to taste it. The sudden release from tension, the friendly faces of my fellow-countrymen and this wonderful meal after the long period of semi-starvation did something to me that the enemy had never been able to do, and I was very near to tears. It seemed incredible that the officers' collars and the tablecloth could be real, as I had not seen anything that had been washed with soap for years.

Captain Williams told me about Huffmeier's behaviour during the liberation of the islands. He had sent a young officer, Captain Zimmerman, on the German surrender ship to rendezvous with Brigadier Snow, who was on board the destroyer Bulldog.

Zimmerman produced a paper authorizing him to receive armistice terms and take them to Admiral Huffmeier. Brigadier Snow made it quite clear that there was no question of an armistice and that Zimmerman would be sent back with a copy of an instrument of surrender — immediate surrender — and arrangements were made for another rendezvous on board *Bulldog*. The young German agreed, but he rose to his feet and announced, 'I am instructed to inform you that your ships must move away from these shores, otherwise Admiral Huffmeier will regard their presence as a breach of faith and a provocative act.' Brigadier Snow was in no mood to listen to this sort of nonsense and promptly ended the interview.

The next rendezvous was at midnight. It appeared that Huffmeier himself was by now terrified of his own troops. He sent a message to Brigadier Snow by his military adviser, Major-General Heine, which read, 'I allowed the English population to fly flags and to hold religious services and therefore had to foresee that a certain agitation might be created among my soldiers. This has happened. I was, and am, therefore in no position to meet you personally.' Such a message from the fanatic Nazi, who less than two weeks before had exhorted his troops to fight to the death, indicated that in common with many other arrogant bullies he was a coward when he himself had to face defeat. Heine also brought with him Huffmeier's authority to sign an unconditional surrender. By the time that all the details had been worked out it was after dawn, which accounted for the delay of twenty-four hours before the British Task Force landed on Guernsey on 10 May. When I reached home I found a letter waiting for me:

Whitehall,
London, S.W.1

10 May 1945

Dear Mrs. Hathaway,

I am very glad to have the opportunity of sending you a message of greeting, to put on record an expression of appreciation, both on the part of the Home Office and of myself, of the courage with which you and your people have faced the trials and privations of the long period of enemy occupation now happily at an end, and to convey to you my best wishes for the future prosperity of the Islands.

We have been very glad to receive in the Home Office some news of you, both from yourself and from your husband in Germany, and I hope you will soon be reunited.

Yours sincerely,
(signed) HERBERT MORRISON.

Now that we were liberated there was one urgent official matter that had to be settled as soon as possible. The Germans had taken it for granted that I, as Dame of Sark, ruled the island, not realising that my husband was actually the Seigneur. Bob and I had agreed that as I spoke German he would remain in the background and I would deal with the Germans. When Bob was deported to Laufen in 1943, he had completely forgotten that he, as the Seigneur, should leave a document appointing me as deputy. I had continued to exercise my authority, trusting to luck that the Germans would not discover that I had no legal right to do so.

Within a few days of our liberation I crossed to Guernsey to appear before the Royal Court in order to legalize all business that had been passed by the Chief Pleas during my husband's absence and to empower me to carry on until such time as he could return. All the business was legalized and I was empowered to act in Bob's capacity until his return.

It was a joy to be able to write real letters to Amice and Jehanne after the five years we had been confined to brief, guarded messages through the Red Cross, many of which had failed to reach their destination. But still there was no news, either by telegram or letter, from Bob, and I began to get very anxious. Later, I found out that Laufen had been liberated by the American Army and all his letters had gone by the American forces mail.

On 7 June King George and Queen Elizabeth visited Guernsey.
Everyone went crazy with delight. We donned our pre-war garments
and got out all the flags that we had kept hidden from the Germans.
I had the privilege of being presented to the King and handing him
a loyal address from Sark. Afterwards I was invited to tea. The King
was very kind about my husband and promised to see that enquiries
were made and his return should be speeded up in every possible
way. During the course of conversation the King told me that the
Russian prisoners who lined the route when he drove through the
island, cheering as lustily as any of the islanders, were the first he had
seen, and he was struck by the different tone of their voices when
cheering. While we were enjoying tea, I took the opportunity to convey the joy and gratitude the people of Sark felt for their Red Cross
parcels and help, and to mention that they had given no less than
£1,187 in collections, which was a large sum for only 363 people
with no trade or tourists to help them. Ten days later I received a
letter from Whitehall dated 14 June 1945.

My dear Dame,

I thought that you might like to know that at a reception of the
International Red Cross which I attended yesterday I mentioned the
various messages of thanks for the Red Cross supplies which I had
been asked to pass on when I was in the Channel Islands last week.

May I take this opportunity of saying how glad I am that it fell
to me to accompany Their Majesties as Minister in Attendance on
such a historic trip and to be able so soon after becoming Home
Secretary to see the Channel Islands in the early days of their liberation from the enemy?

I was very glad to have had the chance of meeting you personally.

(signed) DONALD SOMERVELL.

Five days after the Royal visit I had a telegram from Bob, who
arrived in London on 18 June (which, incidentally, was Jehanne's
birthday) and took the first available flight to Guernsey, where he

arrived 21 June. The moment I caught sight of him at the harbour I realised that he must not guess from my expression how his appearance shook me. He had always been a lean man; now he was nothing more than a bag of bones. He had the unhealthy pallor of a man who has been cooped up inside a prison for a long time, and he looked as if he was still suffering from a high degree of nervous tension. Although I had taken every possible care to look my best when we met, there was a niggling worry at the back of my mind that he might find my appearance far from pleasing. My weight had dropped from ten stone to seven, and there were revolting hollows under my cheekbones, which made me look remarkably grim. In spite of our wonderful reunion he remained terribly thin and nervy for several months.

Jehanne came to Sark at the beginning of July and two weeks later my eldest daughter, Amice, came back to Guernsey. I crossed over to meet her, not only for the pleasure of it but to try to soften her distress at seeing what the German troops had done to her house, 'La Cour de Longue'. All the furniture had been completely wrecked; the drawers of chests and tallboys taken away, and nothing but the frames left. Her silver, which was hidden in the roof, had been discovered and stolen. Fortunately, her Baby Austin car had been concealed in a haystack by her faithful cowman, but it was a sorry sight. Finally, after a most depressing tour of the house, we returned to the sitting-room and sat on a packing-case. Amice gazed about her with a rather woebegone expression, then looked up with a smile and said, 'well, at least they have left the blinds,' and went over to pull one down. The moment she did so she was confronted with a mass of pornographic drawings, decorated with swastikas and eagles.

Every house which had been occupied by German troops was left in a filthy state, and the air was permeated by the stench of polluted W.C. pans, mixed with a sickly smell of cheap scent which was used by low-grade Germans, presumably in order to disguise the smell of their unwashed bodies. Amice refused to be downhearted by these problems. She moved into her house with a borrowed table, chair and oil lamp. Jehanne went over to help her, and for several weeks they worked together, scrubbing floors, washing walls, disinfecting bathrooms, and getting the house ready for her family's return. We found material for curtains, kitchen equipment, and a sufficient amount of furniture for her needs. Meanwhile, I was forced to stay in Sark because there were crowds of officials arriving on the island, and I had to be there to greet them. We were visited by men from the Ministry of Health who wanted to examine the condition of our children, and by Army, Navy and Air Force officials, both British and American. I asked one American colonel why it had taken so long to capture Cherbourg, and was rather startled when he said, 'well, it was partly the fault of one Julius Caesar who built a rampart across the peninsula, which the Germans had concreted and used as a sort of Maginot Line.'

CHAPTER 12

PEACE-TIME EXPERIMENTS

Now that the war was over, we had to set about the business of the rehabilitation of Sark, no trifling matter after five years of enemy occupation. There were 13,500 mines to be cleared off our land, over an area only three and a half miles long and one and a half miles wide. Our roads had been left in a shocking state by the Germans, who had brought over not only cars but two French Whippet tanks. German prisoners were kept on the island for eight months to work under the Royal Engineers in order to clear the mines and resurface the roads.

We had to have a new doctor and new schoolteachers, which entailed a great deal of correspondence for me, as I have to vet their applications. And something had to be done to encourage the children; so I evolved a system by which their school fees would be paid by the island if, having passed a standard required by the College or Grammar School in Guernsey, they were willing to go there and attend. All the houses that had been occupied by the Germans had to be repaired and redecorated.

Another urgent problem was how to get our new harbour completed. Work had started on this in 1936 and we had sufficient funds to complete it at the original contracted prices, but work had had to be closed down at the beginning of the war owing to our inability to obtain the necessary materials. When we restarted work in 1946 the post-war cost was nearly double that of the pre-war contract.

When we applied to the Home Office for help for the Island we were told that we could use the balance which we had earmarked for the harbour and invested in War Loan, toward the cost of rehabilitation. I felt that this was a dishonest economy on the part of the

Home Office because the money we had saved for the harbour had taken years to accumulate and had been put aside for the express purpose of building our new harbour: therefore it should be used for no other purpose. The Landing tax paid by visitors for some thirty years past had been accumulated on the understanding that it was for our most important project, and Sark had shown a patriotic spirit by investing this money in War Loan. I wrote a firm letter to Mr. Markbreiter at the Home Office, telling him plainly that if we used our fund for any other purpose we should be copying the British Government's tactics with their Motor Car Taxes, and I flatly refused to do this. We were then politely told that as we were the only island to emerge from the war with a credit balance nothing would be done to help us. This seemed a harsh policy, as proportionally we had suffered just as much as the other islands and invested what money we had in the War Effort. However, I am glad to say that the National Provincial Bank immediately gave us a loan on very easy terms, and we can pride ourselves on having solved our difficulties without any outside grants. The loan gave us a satisfactory feeling of independence, and we no longer had to go cap in hand to the Home Office.

The final cost of our harbour was £52,000 — a considerable sum of money for an island of some five hundred inhabitants to produce. During my acrimonious' correspondence with the Home Office I worked out an ambitious plan for the opening of our harbour, but this plan I kept to myself. If my hope materialized, Sark would enjoy a great deal of well-deserved publicity. However, it would be wise to wait for a couple of years until the work was complete before making any move. I bided my time.

Meanwhile, Bob's family and our friends in the U.S.A. were anxious to see us after nearly six years of war, but it was not possible for me to get away until 1946, because the work kept me busy all day long and far into the night for many months. Eventually Bob and I sailed in the *Queen Elizabeth*. As we were strictly rationed at home it was a gourmet's life for us from the moment we left Southampton, and I will never forget the sight of the first really white rolls I had

The Royal couple in one of the island's horse-drawn carriages

179

My drawing-room—the fireplace was made from a
four-poster bed.

seen since 1939, juicy steaks, and meat served with every meal. The dining-room stewards seemed so anxious to make up for the lean years of war rations that they were quite disappointed when a second helping was refused.

Friends of ours, whom we met in America later told us that they had crossed over in the *Queen Mary* that month on her last voyage trooping G.I. brides for the American Army. Lord Woolton, the Minister of Food, was on board and he wrote out a message for the brides which was published in the *Atlantic Times*. Our friends had kept the message, which I think is worth repeating. It read:

'GREETINGS FROM LORD WOOLTON

'I want to wish all G.I. brides good luck. It's a great adventure on which you are engaged. Christopher Columbus had a worse passage than you have had. You will find many people in America who will tell you that their people came over in the Mayflower. It was a small ship. You are making history on a bigger scale. In five hundred years' time, people will say with pride: "My people came over on the *Queen Mary*." You will be an ancestor.

'If you do your job properly, you will help to make the Americans understand the British, and to like us, because they like you. And I hope you will tell your people at home all that is good about America. It is a great country; ours is a great country too . . . and the peace of the world depends upon us knowing and respecting one another.

'The G.I. brides, over sixty thousand of them, may be a grand missionary army, bringing understanding between the two countries. But wherever you are, I wish you happiness in your homes and prosperity in your work.'

We were told that when the two thousand English brides arrived at the dock the scene of reunion with their husbands was unforgettable. The husbands were held behind a barrier so high that they could not see over it. This was necessary because when the barrier had been low enough to see over they had broken it down in a mad rush to get to the women. The name of each G.I. bride was called out and the door of the barrier was opened to let her husband through. Then each dashed across the intervening space into the other's arms. We were told that some of them did not recognise one another, and it was rather pathetic to see them hesitate and look a little bewildered as they first caught sight of their partners. A Red Cross girl was posted to take charge of any baby carried by the bride when the meeting took place, and one couple actually fainted simultaneously as they kissed. The bride swooned into the arms of the Red Cross girl, and her husband passed out with a bang at the feet of the sergeant standing by. They were both carried off on stretchers. There were no such dramatic scenes when the *Queen Elizabeth* docked at Pier 90.

We spent Christmas in Boston at the Ritz with the Hathaway family. It was the first real high, wide and careless holiday we had known for seven years. We wandered up Beacon Hill into the little streets where the houses have charming ironwork balconies and transoms over the doors. All the doors were left wide open, and the windows brightly lit, each with a row of seven or more candles.

After the New Year I began an extensive lecture tour, and in March I went to Canada, where I was to speak at the Royal Ontario Museum. Hardly had I started when I was attacked by laryngitis. Fortunately Bob was sitting next to me, so I handed him my notes and croaked in his ear: 'Take over — I've lost my voice.' Bob grabbed the notes but paid them no heed. Instead of following the copy he produced some hilarious remark of his own for every scene shown in the film. The following morning my lecture was reported in one of the papers and Bob was described as 'a new star with a wit as dry as paper'.

After this lecture we went to stay with the Robert Weavers on their ranch in Arizona, and a few days of sunshine cured my laryngitis. We moved from the Weavers to Cleveland where I lectured at the City Hall and the Cleveland Museum of Art. During our visit I was impressed by the astonishing swing away from isolation which had taken place since 1939. But the American attitude towards the British amused me. They still had a firm belief that life in England was starchy and snobbish, and were quite unaware of the fact that we had progressed towards democracy to a far greater degree than they had. They themselves were still busy building up tradition and in many cases were far more snobbish than we are. This was particularly noticeable in the upper-crust attitude towards Jews.

We spent a few days in New York before sailing for home. Since our last visit the old elevated railways had disappeared and the city looked even more glittering with prosperity than I had remembered it. Miles of sheet glass sparkled in the sun-swept avenues, and window displays along Fifth Avenue were like gay herbaceous borders. It seemed incredible that shoppers could buy whatever they wanted without coupons, and that nothing was rationed.

The morning after our arrival I went window-shopping and stood spellbound before a candy store, gazing at trays heaped high with delicately coloured fondants, chocolates cased in heavy gold and silver paper and boxes of candy tied with double-backed satin ribbon. Then I spent a dream-like half-hour in Elizabeth Arden's, buying creams, lotions, make-up and boxes of bulky pink sweet-smelling rose geranium soap — everything beautifully packed and actually wrapped in paper!

We returned home at the end of March and were encouraged by the good spirits and optimism in Sark. Preparations were in full swing for the coming season, when the tourist trade would start again for the first time since 1939. We were not disappointed in our hopes — accommodation at the hotels was all booked up and day trippers flocked to the island to see how we had fared during the Occupation.

During the holiday season a prominent member of the new Labour Government turned up in Sark. Bob had the greatest distrust of this particular man and, moreover, thought it a waste of the British taxpayer's money that planes and M.T.B.'s should be laid on for him and his family on a holiday which had no connection with government business.

The atmosphere was definitely strained when I insisted that the couple must be invited to dinner, though I had no more wish to entertain them than Bob had. Nevertheless, it is the business of the Seigneur to entertain all notable visitors to the island regardless of personal opinions.

The party was chosen with care and were told on no account to bring up controversial matters. All went well until I spoke of my recent visit to America, whereupon our guest proceeded to say how much he wished that we had Roosevelt in England and the Americans had Churchill. This was too much for me, and I told him that, judging by the public applause that greeted Churchill on the cinema newsreels in the United States, I was quite sure that the Americans would be only too happy to support his idea.

Jehanne announced her engagement to Harry Bell that summer, and the wedding was planned to take place the following spring. Harry had been a very keen sportsman. He was a Cambridge Soccer Blue and played for England against Wales and Belgium. During the war he became GSO3 and GSO2 on the staff of the Northern Command Headquarters, while Jehanne had served with the A.T.S. and with the Channel Islands Division of the Red Cross at Clarence House. Much to my joy, Jehanne and Harry had decided to make their home in Sark, and bought a property at Bel Air.

In December I went back to America — this time alone — to carry out a much more extensive lecture tour which lasted until March and took me from Minneapolis in the north to Texas in the south and from New York to California. Once again I spent Christmas in Arizona with the Weavers.

My hostess at Houston, where I was giving a lecture, was Mrs. Wirt Paddock, and I had an amusing experience one morning when the Wirt chauffeur drove me round the city to show me the sights. His accent was strange, but somehow seemed familiar, so I asked him where he came from. When he said that he was of Acadian French descent from Louisiana I remembered having been told many years before that a great number of French inhabitants also had been deported to Nova Scotia in 1775, had worked their way down to Louisiana and had preserved their old Norman French, Which was said to be the same as our Sark *patois* and that of French Canada. I suddenly asked him in his own tongue how it was that big ships could come to Houston as I had seen no signs of the ocean there. He was so surprised and delighted that I could speak his language that we continued the conversation in our respective ancient dialects. Then he took me to see the famous port of Houston and the man-made basin where the ships turn round.

When I got back to New York, before sailing I spent my time shopping to collect a trousseau and household materials for Jehanne. It was a delightful orgy, unhampered by coupons or rations, and my family and friends cooperated with enthusiasm. One friend actually gave me a Whole hundredweight of sugar for the wedding cake and refreshments. Oddly enough, this gift nearly reduced me to tears, for I had never dreamed of seeing so much sugar again in my life. I was able to buy all the fruit and other ingredients for the cake. Over and above this I bought yards of material for the wedding dress, lingerie and cretonne, and a lovely wedding veil. No less than twenty-seven bulky packages were delivered on board the Queen Mary when I sailed for home.

Jehanne met me at Southampton. At that time it was extremely difficult to obtain a pass to go on board when the ships docked, but as I had been suffering from an acute attack of sciatica she had received permission to help me land. When we checked over our luggage at the customs shed I was horrified to find I had left Jehanne's wedding veil in a box under the bed in my cabin. To her dismay I hopped gaily over the customs bench, dashed back up the gangway, and retrieved the missing box. It was quite astonishing how that wedding veil cured the last twinges of sciatica.

While I was in America Bob had entertained Field-Marshal Montgomery for lunch. The Field-Marshal had seen fit to bring along a photographer and after lunch insisted on having a photograph taken with all the staff outside the house. As the staff were in the middle of washing up they were far from pleased with this idea, but when the honoured guest refused to accept their polite excuses they reluctantly came to the front door and donned their society smiles. The following week, a large mounted photograph arrived signed 'To the staff of La Seigneurie'. Bob told me it was received very coldly, and he was given to understand that it was just as well that all notable guests did not make a habit of this sort of thing.

The islanders wondered whether the Field-Marshal's visit might be connected with persuading us to join the National Military Service, and whether he realised that the Channel Islands were never in point of fact part of England, but part and parcel of the Duchy of Normandy, and as such no doubt took part in the Norman Conquest of England, becoming thereby an appanage of the Crown of England. Very many English people do not understand that to us the Sovereign of England is the successor of the Dukes of Normandy, and we who have been part of that Duchy are devotedly loyal to the Crown as Channel Islanders rather than English people.

For many years the Channel Islands had their own compulsory militia service. I have an old side-drum to remind us that the Royal Sark Militia was loyal to the Stuart King in Cromwellian days, and their badge was an S surrounded by oak leaves. This drum is still used, but in a more domestic fashion than in the days of old. It is kept in my front hall and serves as a gong to warn my house guests that meals are ready.

Sark, by the way, was very materially affected by the Civil War in England. Guernsey ranged itself on the side of Cromwell, and Jersey on the side of the King. Sark naturally followed Jersey because the de Carterets, who had been Seigneurs of Sark since the days of Queen Elizabeth, came from Jersey and were all ardent Royalists. During this time Sark was occupied and held by troops from Guernsey and such revenue as there was went to the Governor of Guernsey, who was a Parliamentarian. This was a severe blow to the de Carterets, who had not only remained faithful to the Royal cause, but had for years sacrificed not only their fortunes but in some cases their lives to the reigning monarch.

After the Battle of Naseby, Charles II, who was then Prince of Wales, came to Jersey where he spent some months during 1646, and the de Carterets again harboured him in 1649 after his father was beheaded. It is good to recall that Charles II, who was often accused of forgetting his friends, showed the de Carteret family many signal marks of favour after he became King, and in 1676 granted a Patent to the Seigneur conferring on him the right to build a pier and collect tolls and duties which had hitherto been payable to the Government. So the de Carteret family were at last rewarded for their services and came into their own again.

Queen Mary spoke of this to me when I had the honour of meeting her while staying with my friend, Mrs. Ionides, in Sussex. She came one day with the Princess Royal for an informal luncheon, and asked me a great many questions about the German Occupation. Though she was nearly eighty years old she had a lively memory of a visit to Guernsey in 1923, and I was amazed at the keen and practical questions she asked about our problems during the war. She even wanted to know how we managed to provide shoes for the growing children.

Meanwhile, plans in Sark were going forward for Jehanne's forthcoming marriage. This wedding was the first that had taken place from the Seigneurie for over two hundred years, and all Sark celebrated the occasion with us. The unconventional atmosphere added greatly to the charm and happiness of the day. After leaving the church the bride and bridegroom were escorted on foot by the British Legion to the Village Hall, where there was tea for four hundred. As a special boat had been run to bring another two hundred guests, including many of the family, from Guernsey, we also had a party at the Seigneurie, and all the island carriages were in use. The bridal pair left the harbour by speedboat for Guernsey, where they were to catch a plane. On their way across they were met and escorted by two other speedboats who attached white ribbons to their boats to form a large V-sign as they came into Guernsey harbour.

One great sadness overshadowed our rejoicings. My eldest daughter, Amice, was suffering from cancer and she died a month after Jehanne's wedding — in fact Jehanne and Harry had to cut short their honeymoon in order to come back for the funeral, which took place in Sark.

Amice's suffering and death caused me more bitterness of heart than anything that has ever happened to me. In many ways she was nearer to me than anyone else in the world. She was always my delight from the time I was eighteen years old and had first held her in my arms. Of all the family she was the most beloved and outstanding personality. From the time she was a baby, Amice had the infectious gift of happiness which made everyone with whom she came into contact devoted to her. She never seemed to have a care in the world, and yet when I look at her photograph now I notice that although she was very pretty, there was something rather pathetic about her expression. She left a son and a daughter to whom I am devoted; both of them are now married and have their own children.

Fortunately for me there was now an urgent matter to take my mind off this family sorrow. Work on our new harbour was finally finished, and the time had now come to attempt the plan I had formulated two years previously in 1946. So I ventured to write to the Duke of Edinburgh's secretary asking him if he would approach the Duke and ascertain whether he would consider coming to open our new harbour. To my delight I received a very gracious reply suggesting that the Duke could come at the end of November or early December. After much thought and hesitation I decided I must point out that during the wintry season there might be a stiff gale from the north-east which would make it impossible to approach our new harbour. Another gracious reply came to the effect that H.R.H. would keep the invitation in mind and fix a date in the following spring. Finally to our great joy I received a letter informing me that a date during the following June of 1949 had been fixed, and the Princess

Elizabeth would accompany the Duke on his visit to Sark. The Chief Pleas was called upon beforehand to appoint special constables and extra finances for decorations, flags and so on.

All plans for any royal visit have to be submitted for approval to Buckingham Palace, Clarence House, St. James's Palace, or wherever the royal residence may be. This was the first time in history that any member of the royal family had visited Sark officially. The only previous occasion had been unofficial, in 1902, when Princess Victoria — sister of King George V — had cruised round the islands in the royal yacht and landed incognito in Sark accompanied by Lady Airlie. While they were on the island a gale sprang up, and it was found impossible to take them off again. An attempt was made to send a boat from the yacht to pick the party up on one of our beaches, but the boat was swamped, and the Princess and her party had to spend the night at the Bel Air Hotel (since destroyed by the Germans). My mother and father respected the Princess's incognito but sent fruit and flowers and a night-dress to the hotel for her use.

Now, forty-seven years later, we were to celebrate our first official royal visit, on Thursday, 23 June, and there was only one great anxiety — would the weather favour us? Even at the height of summer a squall may suddenly blow up between Guernsey and Sark, and if this happened it was more than probable that the visit would not take place.

Weatherwise, the day started in surly fashion, clouds massing in a grey sky and a vicious look over the face of the waters. Princess Elizabeth and the Duke of Edinburgh were on board *Anson*, escorted by destroyers *Roebuck* and *Wizard*. When they were a mile or so east of our Le Creux harbour *Anson* announced over her loud-speaking system that she was proceeding to Guernsey, which made the people of Sark fear that the weather had done its damnedest and scuppered their great expectations. But in spite of the choppy sea, we were not to be disappointed. The order was given that Their Royal Highnesses would visit Sark by M.T.B. as soon as *Anson* dropped anchor in Guernsey roads, and two M.T.B.s sped out of port towards the island. The first took oft newspaper representatives, B.B.C. stall and cameramen. The second embarked the royal party. Children and spectators were packed in the harbour's narrow confines.

Bob and I, with the Sénéschal and Prévôt, were in our places as the M.T.B. carrying the royal party arrived at the harbour steps. The Princess had some difficulty in landing, because the boat was still rocking, but after a moment's hesitation she made up her mind to jump for it. As she did so, she all but slipped. It was a terrible moment for those of us who were watching, but the Government Secretary, Major-General R. F. Colwill, who was standing on the steps, caught her just in time. She recovered at once, and followed by the Duke and the royal party came up the steps to the quayside where we were waiting to be presented. By now the grey skies had given way and there was a warm, sunny welcome for the Princess, who looked enchanting in a summery lemon dress and jacket.

After the band had played the National Anthem, Bob, as Seigneur, read the Loyal Address:

'We, the Seigneur, Seneschal and Prévôt of the Island of Sark, with our Humble Duty, ask leave to express to Your Royal Highness the joy of the Chief Pleas and People of Sark on the occasion of this, your first visit, and to say how great and sincere is the welcome which we extend to you.

'In this Island, granted in 1565 by Her Gracious Majesty, the Queen Elizabeth of happy memory, to Helier de Carteret, Lord of the Seigneurie of Saint Ouen in the Island of Jersey, the laws and customs then prevailing have continued substantially unaltered to the present time, and we would not have it otherwise, for we believe that they serve our purpose and meet our needs.

'We yield to none in our loyalty to the Crown and in our affection for members of your Royal House, and we humbly pray that the blessing of Almighty God may always rest upon 'Your Royal Highnesses and upon your son, the Prince Charles.'

The Princess replied in these words:

'I thank the Seigneur, Seneschal and Prévôt of Sark, and, through them, the People of the Island, for their welcome to us on this, our first visit to the Channel Islands.

'We know what unfaltering loyalty they have shown to the Crown, in times of adversity no less than in happier days, and today we have received personal experience of their affection for us and for our son.

'We, for our part, shall always take interest in whatever affects the welfare of the Island and the good of its inhabitants. May God be with you.'

Next I asked the Duke formally to open the Maseline Harbour. In the course of his short speech he mentioned that it was due to my having invited him to perform this ceremony that the whole visit to the Channel Islands had resulted. Whether this came as a surprise to the officials of Guernsey and Jersey, I have no idea, but it certainly came as a delightful surprise to me that the Duke should have paid me the compliment of it publicly.

There was one little incident which was typical of the informality and homeliness of Sark. While Bob was reading the Loyal Address a small mongrel ran out of the crowd and advanced with an air of calm confidence towards the Princess, who gave him a friendly pat. This he acknowledged with a wagging tail and retired once more into the crowd.

After the official ceremony was over the royal party walked through the tunnel to the road beyond it where the carriages were drawn up. The crowd cheered. All the children waved flags vigorously and the Duke inspected the Sark branch of the British Legion. Then the royal couple were ushered into the first open victoria, driven by Charlie Perree. To judge from their smiling faces as they took their seats, they seemed to be looking forward to the drive. The Princess's Comptroller and her Lady-in-Waiting rode in the second carriage, while the Duke's Equerry sat on the seat next to John Baker, who was driving. Bob and I, with the rest of the party, followed in other carriages.

It is a steep climb up the road from the harbour to Bel Air. Frank Baker, the Constable, with his mace of office, and Special Constable Harry Carre walked beside the royal carriage. As the carriage toiled up the hill the Duke kept up a lively conversation with Frank Baker, and every now and then looked back to grin at his Equerry perched on the box of the following victoria. Charlie Perree had the rare distinction of driving royalty, for this must have been one of the few occasions when they were not driven by their own coachmen or chauffeurs. Another homely touch was provided by one of the Princess's detectives solemnly leading the second horse, while his companion walked beside him. Along the road to the Seigneurie bunches of flowers were tossed into the carriages by bystanders, and as the procession passed our church bells rang a welcome. A few minutes later the carriages rolled down to the Seigneurie, where Princess Elizabeth's personal standard was flying from the tower.

Here we had a private luncheon, a small party of fourteen which included Princess Elizabeth's Lady-in-Waiting, Lady Alice Egerton, the Home Secretary, Mr. Chuter Ede, Sir Frederick Browning, Lieutenant Michael Parker and my daughter, Jehanne Bell, with her husband. When present, royalty always sit as host and hostess.

On this occasion I had sent to America for a real Virginia ham and all the 'trimmings' — sweet potatoes, pineapple, wild rice and pickled peaches. I may say the cost of air postage was far greater than the cost of the ham and all the accessories. The meal also included our young and tenderest lobsters cooked in a special way with our delicious cream.

After luncheon, while we were sitting in the drawing-room, someone must have mentioned the little mongrel at the harbour, for the Princess suddenly said to me: 'I have heard about your poodle, but I haven't yet seen her.' As a matter of fact Bella, my large white standard poodle, had been shut in an upstairs room and had not been groomed for royalty. I had been so occupied with the preparations for the visit that I had neglected Bella's toilet, which involves at least half an hour's hard work and necessitates large sheets spread on the floor, a wire brush and clippers. (I always clip Bella myself, and have a book demonstrating all the various styles of poodle cuts.) However, I sent for her, and as she loves company she did not disgrace me. She enjoys publicity like a film star, and every Monday, when my gardens are open to sightseers, makes it her business to pose for snapshots alongside my white pigeons.

The visiting journalists expressed the opinion that this was the most enjoyable royal visit they had ever reported, and were delighted with the informality which contrasted strongly with most royal visits.

An alternative route was chosen for the drive back to the old Le Creux harbour where the party arrived at three o'clock prior to departure.

Six years after our Liberation, German uniforms were to be seen once again in Sark while *Appointment with Venus* was being filmed. This was a silly but rather charming story by Jerrard Tickell about an imaginary commando raid on the island to rescue a pedigree Guernsey cow in 1940, in which the leading parts were played by David Niven, Glynis johns, Kenneth More and Barry Jones.

Barry Jones was a Guernseyman and very popular in Sark because he had commanded a platoon of Sark men in France during the 1914 War. He enjoyed himself so much on location that he stayed on for a few days after the rest of the company left. Although he owned a house in London, the lure of the island was so strong that he remained until the last moment to supervise repairs on a cottage he had bought in Guernsey sixteen years before.

David Niven was an old friend of ours — in fact, we had last seen him in America when we were visiting Nora and Lefty Flynn on their plantation in Carolina. I remember that visit well because it was my first to the Deep South, and one incident has stuck in my mind ever since. The Negro groom was dressed in very shabby livery. One day David said to him, 'I've got a pair of shoes that I think you might be able to wear. What size do you take?' To my astonishment the young fellow's reply was: 'Ah doan know what size ah taks, suh. Ah ain never haid new shoes.'

One of David Niven's most charming characteristics is that he never seems to take himself seriously, and his amusing stories are always against himself. Before the war we had laughed at his descriptions of the long, long trail that led him from Sandhurst to Hollywood, how Lieutenant Niven had joined the Highland Light Infantry and served in Malta for two years, then decided that peace-time soldiering offered little adventure and so wrote an admirable concise note to his commanding officer which read:

'Dear Colonel,
    Request permission to resign commission.
                    Love
                        Niven.'

This was followed by a gay six months in Canada working first of all on a newspaper, then on bridge construction, then as a waiter and then as a barman. David told us how he became the first salesman to be employed by Jack and Charlie of the famous '21' Restaurant in New York when they became respectable wine merchants after prohibition ended. He was forced to resign that job as a result of a confidence trick by a person or persons unknown, who put through a call asking for fifty cases of special wine to be delivered at the Café Marguery — a select joint patronized by 'lovely prominent people'. The cases were delivered with all speed and unloaded by white-coated characters on the sidewalk, and a cheque was handed to the truck-driver, who drove off. It was then a matter of minutes before a second truck drove up, reloaded the cases and drove away to a destination unknown. The cheque bounced, and so did the young salesman's job after an interview with Jack and Charlie who had been equally fooled by the 'con' men.

During a visit to Peru, where as usual a revolution was in progress and it seemed to be a free-for-all, David joined in — on both sides.

But the fun and games ended when the British Consul gave him twenty minutes to get out of the country, whence he eventually landed in Hollywood.

When we first met him he was already a top-line film star. His Swedish wife had come over with him while the film was on location in Sark, and one night when they were dining with us I happened to complain about a man who was causing me a good deal of trouble.

'But why do you not get rid of him?' she asked.

I enquired if she had any suggestions to offer. The answer I got was: 'Oh, I think it is quite easy. In my country they say that if you hang a mackerel in the moonlight for two nights, then serve it to your enemy, he will be dead in a few days.' Bob remarked that in future he would eye mackerel served at the table with grave mistrust.

After dinner the talk turned — as it often does in Sark — to treasure troves, and I told the story about one of the Seigneurs of the le Pelley family who is said to have hidden his silver during the Napoleonic wars and died later without telling anybody where he had buried it. One day a great friend of mine who was staying with me had said she had heard there was a clairvoyant staying in the island, and suggested that I might get her to the Seigneurie for a séance. We decided to tell no one of our plan, and I got the woman to come to the Seigneurie on an evening I knew my friend and I would be alone. When the clairvoyant arrived I explained about the silver and she asked if it would be possible for her to hold something which had belonged to the old le Pelley. I produced a letter written by him to his mother in 1810. She held this against her forehead for a while, appeared to go into a trance and announced that she was following two men carrying a box and they were pushing it into a hole in the side of a steep bank. Then, without a word of warning, she dashed out of the house saying we must find five trees. My friend and I pursued her and searched about in the dark till we found five trees growing out of one stump near a chapel at the side of the house. . . .

Here Bob interrupted my story by saying, 'Believe it or not, Sibyl had holes dug all round and under that tree. Needless to say, nothing was found, but Jehanne was convinced that the silver would be unearthed near the house, and soon after the war a Sapper friend of hers came to stay with us and the two of them went over the whole area with a mine detector. The detector did its job all right, and they unearthed one horseshoe and a few old tins.'

Our guests looked as disgusted as if they had been cheated, and someone said plaintively, 'It wouldn't have ended that way in a film script.'

Appointment with Venus brought much publicity to Sark, and, though the story seemed piffle to me, I was anxious that a really good cow should be chosen to play the part of Venus. Fortunately she turned out to be an adequate Guernsey, born and bred on a Guernsey farm. Poor cow — she had to suffer for her stardom. She was transported from Guernsey to Sark where she was forced to climb our high cliff paths, go to sea in a motor torpedo boat, calve in a cave under the fierce glare of arc-lights and then voyage to England, where it is to be hoped that she was allowed to settle down to a quiet life.

CHAPTER 13

WELCOME AND UNWELCOME VISITORS

Three years slipped by very pleasantly and in May 1954 Bob's brother and his wife came over to visit us. We met them in Paris and had a wonderfully happy motor tour with them through France and Spain. By the time we were on our way back Bob was showing signs of being easily tired and complained of a pain in his leg. The doctor frightened me by his diagnosis of thrombosis, but said that the condition was not sufficiently acute to cause alarm and, if I could prevent Bob from getting overtired and he took things quietly, the inflammation of the vein would probably subside. Stewart, Helen and I tried to keep him from doing too much and this was easy enough once we got back to Sark. By the time Stewart and Helen went back to America, Bob had no more pain and said he felt fine, but I was not entirely happy about him. He seemed to have aged.

We were looking forward to our next royal visit, which took place in the second week of July, when the Duke and Duchess of Gloucester came to our annual cattle show. The Duke was that year's President of the English Guernsey Cattle Society, and as he has a fine herd himself at Barnwell he appreciated the good points of a Guernsey cow.

The royal party arrived in the morning and, after an official welcome at the harbour, a procession of carriages toiled up the hill to Bel Air and trundled along the flat country road on the island's high table-top three hundred and fifty feet above the sea, then turned into our drive. Before lunch we served champagne cocktails and the day's programme had been arranged to allow enough time for a stroll around the Seigneurie gardens before driving to the show-field where the presentation of cups took place. The Duke knew, of course, that our island cattle are, in all cases, pedigree animals entered in the

Guernsey Herd Book and equal to the average standard of that breed anywhere.

Many people who are not breeders find this hard to believe and are also under the impression that an Alderney cow is not a Guernsey. This is assumed because Alderney had its own Herd Book. Cattle breeders know that all the Channel Islands cattle are descended from the Isigny and Froment de Leon breeds of Normandy.

After the presentations, there was a drive back to the harbour where the royal party embarked for Guernsey. For us in Sark it had been a lovely day. The Duke left an impression of friendly interest and kindness in all our minds and the Duchess made us feel that she had really enjoyed the informality of the occasion. A few days later I received two letters which pleased Bob as much as they pleased me. One was from the Duke's Equerry saying that Their Royal Highnesses were enchanted not only with our home, but with the island as a whole. The other came from the Lieutenant Governor, Sir Thomas Elmhirst, who wrote: 'The Duke and Duchess were delighted with their visit to Sark. I do thank you and your husband for all the arrangements which went to make the day such a success. The programme was, I think, just as it should have been and all the better for giving us time to walk round the garden and the excellent champagne cocktails before your delicious luncheon. We had a good trip back and were on the air field at 5 p.m., just in time, as the weather closed it down shortly after.' I was still worried about Bob, and in October I persuaded him to go to Switzerland to see a specialist in Lausanne. We had kept a car in France for some years and only had to make a short flight to Dinard, where we picked up the car and drove by easy stages to Lausanne. From there we went on to Germany, where Bob wanted to see Schloss Laufen where he had been a prisoner for two and a half years. By now it had been turned into a home for old folks and was gay with curtains and window-boxes full of flowers. Bob stared at the building in dead silence for some time, then said bitterly, 'Doubtless the old folks appreciate all the care that has been taken to turn this into a haven of rest, but I can't help wondering if the interior is still as bug-infested as it was in our day.'

After this rather grim pilgrimage we went on to see two of our former German Commandants who had both been very kind to us during the Occupation. Our first call was on Baron von Aufsess, whose stark and primitive Schloss is in Schwabia. He and his wife took us to Schloss Greifenstein to meet the von Stauffenbergs, whose relative Colonel Count Claus von Stauffenberg made a courageous attempt to blow up Hitler in 1944. Ten years had gone by since then and on this sunny autumn afternoon, 1944 seemed far away and long ago, but the memories of those days would remain with us as long as we lived. For each of us the nightmare memories differed. Baron von Aufsess's wife had been in a concentration camp for speaking against Hitler. Though von Aufsess himself had continued to hold command in the Channel Islands, he had been in bad odour with the Supreme Command. The von Stauffenberg family had suffered the penalties of Hitler's wrath. Bob had been imprisoned at Laufen and I had struggled on in Sark. Yet we had one fortunate thing in common — our homes were still standing and our husbands had survived.

After this Bob and I drove on to Prince Oettingen's lovely home. As I have already mentioned, he had done all he could for us in 1942 when the deportations were ordered and as a result had incurred Hitler's displeasure. Now he welcomed us with great courtesy and took us to see another castle he owns at Harburg with a very famous library, which contains an eighth-century Irish missal and some magnificent Nüremberg carved wood saints and madonnas. Prince Oettingen had been ordered by Hitler to blow up this fabulous building so that it should fall on the road below and delay the advance of General Patton's army. By delaying tactics he was able to prevent this act of desperation, and so saved Schloss Harburg.

From Germany we drove on to Luxembourg, passing the U. S. military cemetery, where General Patton is buried, and Bastogne, which after D-Day was held by the U.S. 101st Airborne Regiment. This was the regiment which had been surrounded by Germans demanding their surrender. The message sent back by the Americans was: 'Nuts.'

We spent two nights in the town of Luxembourg and had the honour of being received by the Grand Duchess Charlotte, a slim, young-looking princess, who talked easily and with great animation in perfect English. Her Lady-in-Waiting was an old friend of mine from Jersey, Lily Le Gallais, who had married a Luxembourgeois. The Grand Duchess's son and heir Prince Jean had served with the Irish Guards. Curiously enough the Luxembourg Army is the only army apart from the British that slopes arms on the left shoulder. They wear British uniforms and were trained by a regimental sergeant-major of the Royal Welch Fusiliers.

We were told that when Hitler first saw the great Adolph Bridge after German troops had occupied Luxembourg in 1940, he assumed that it had been re-named after him, until the burgomaster informed him that it had always had that name.

As Bob's leg seemed to be increasingly painful, I decided that we must fly back to London to consult Sir Horace Evans, and we returned to Sark at the end of October, by which time I was desperately worried.

A few days after our homecoming, we celebrated our Silver wedding Anniversary — 5 November 1954 — by giving a party for all the people of the island. The party started at five o'clock, and each guest was received, first by me and then by Bob. The inhabitants presented us with a Georgian inkstand and Bob made what I did not then realise was to be his last speech to them. I like to remember the way he began it . . . 'I shall not call you Ladies and Gentlemen, but just my friends, for you have given me your friendship which I have valued for twenty-five years.'

As a rule, Bob was a man of few words, but on this occasion he let himself go and as I watched our guests I realised how delighted they were. He left no doubt in their minds of his love for Sark and his genuine interest in every islander.

After the speeches had been made, we asked our guests to continue the party while we went off around the island to take a portion of wedding cake and a glass of wine to all the old and infirm who were unable to attend the celebration. This would have been no mean feat on an ordinary day, but to set out on a bleak wet November afternoon was a self-imposed task which I felt would be too much for Bob's health. I would not let him come back to the Hall but insisted that he should go home while I rejoined our guests, who were still dancing. I gave Bob's regrets and apologies, but everyone knew that he was far from well.

Five weeks later he suddenly collapsed one morning and though he recovered enough to come downstairs again and was able to talk very cheerfully over the transatlantic telephone to his brother, he had a relapse and died ten days before Christmas.

When any member of a Sark family dies, the death is immediately announced from house to house by one of the family friends, and I followed this custom when Bob died. His coffin was carried from the house to the church by members of the 'Douzaine', which consists of twelve men elected by the Chief Pleas from among themselves, forming a sort of Cabinet, or Committee of the Assembly.

A day or two after Bob's funeral, I received a letter of condolence from Buckingham Palace, which was signed by Sir Michael Adeane, Private Secretary to Her Majesty The Queen, and read:

> Buckingham Palace
> 17th December 1954
>
> Dear Mrs. Hathaway,
>
> The Queen desires me to tell you how very much grieved she was yesterday to learn of the death of your husband the Seigneur of Sark.
>
> Her Majesty, who has the happiest recollections of her visit to Sark when she was Princess Elizabeth and of your kindness to her, sends you her deepest sympathy in your loss.
>
> Yours sincerely,
> M. E. Adeane.

As I was three years older than Bob I had never for a moment thought I would outlive him. His death meant another readjustment which was only made bearable for me by Jehanne and her husband living in Sark and giving me every possible help. I decided to leave Jehanne to act as my deputy and get away at once to stay with one of my oldest and best friends, also a widow, who at that time was living in Tunisia.

It was my fourth visit to Hammamet, where Mrs. Richardson Francis had a lovely villa and gardens on the coast. Nothing could have been better for me that particular Christmas, so unlike home. There a number of Europeans and Americans have built villas and, though they were full of quarrels among themselves, they were all exceedingly kind and hospitable to me. Archaeologically, Tunisia is a fascinating country and one longs to see more research done and excavations undertaken. The Moslem city of Kairouan, which is considered to be one of the holiest, contrasts strangely with the Roman Tebourba and the splendid coliseum of El Djem.

I have always taken an interest in food and there is a very special Tunisian dish which is one of the best in my experience. It is called a 'brique' and consists of an absolutely perfect poached egg encased in the lightest and flakiest of pastry. How the egg gets inside the pastry at the exact moment of cooking and then is baked without being overdone remains a mystery to me.

The weather was not good that winter and it was very cold at night. The best season there, as I know it, is May when there are masses of wild flowers and wonderful blue fields of linseed, looking like lakes in the distance. During August the humidity is too great and vast numbers of 'Portuguese men-of-war' make sea-bathing impossible, but my friend had a swimming pool in her garden. As usual, I collected seeds and plants to take back with me for my own garden.

Jehanne and Harry welcomed me home. It is a wonderful thing for me to have them living on the island. Hardly a day goes by that one or the other doesn't come to see me. Since the war, Jehanne has acted as my deputy when I have been away, and Harry is also a

Member of the Chief Pleas, so naturally both have an intimate knowledge of the island's affairs. The social life of Sark does not appeal to them, but they are always with me on official occasions, or when I entertain Royalty.

That very charming and gracious lady the Princess Royal came to Sark in the spring of 1956. It was a May day and she was able to see the wild flowers at their best. After lunch at the Seigneurie, we drove round the island, and she was delighted by the Coupée. In a letter of thanks, she referred to my 'enchanted island' and said that nothing could be more romantic than to see the cliffs of Sark grow from the horizon. The carriage drive past the sheets of violets and primroses seemed to thrill her and so did my garden, which was looking at its best just then.

A few days later, I sent Her Royal Highness some double violets and primroses, and received a letter from her Lady-in-Waiting, telling me how pleased she was and that the Head Gardener at Harewood reported that they had found a new home in the rock garden, where primroses did particularly well. Later, I had the experience of receiving one of the few unwelcome guests who has ever called on me. This was the German Major-General Muller, who for some reason best known to himself had decided to re-visit the Islands, and What was even more strange, expected to be cordially received. He arrived with his sister at my house one morning, and there was nothing for it but to invite him in for a glass of sherry. He kept on saying that he was astonished to see the remarkable prosperity of the Channel Islands. I replied that they had always been prosperous before the Germans came and it was not surprising that they had recovered. Then he tried to be tactful and told me how much younger I was looking than when he last saw me, to which I retorted with some asperity that, considering the troubled negotiations in which I was always involved with him in those days, it was to be expected. It did not seem to occur to the General that his presence was not welcome. He stayed on so long, I thought he would never go. So I suggested that as he had signed my book officially — as all the generals did during their Occupation visits — he had better sign it again, and we walked out into the hall. Even this manoeuvre did not work. He proceeded to give me a commentary on all the German Commandants whose names were there.

CHAPTER 14

THE QUEEN'S VISIT

The greatest event in our island's history took place in 1957: the visit of our Queen. This was the first time a reigning monarch had ever landed in Sark.

I was informed previously by the Governor of Guernsey of the proposed visit. A programme was suggested by the Chief Pleas and funds were voted for re-decorating the school where the sessions of the Chief Pleas were held; red carpets, flags and flowers, and souvenirs for every child plus a tea party later in the day at the Village Hall. A committee was formed to organise the day's events and to select the carriage in which the Queen and Prince Philip would drive. This task was made easy by our holding a Horse Show in May and choosing the prize-winning turn-out. Whenever Royalty comes to Sark, the Chief Pleas is called upon beforehand to appoint special constables and extra finances.

All plans for the visit had to be submitted to Buckingham Palace, and we had to prepare a professionally drawn schedule showing the positions of island officials (Seneschal, Prévôt and Greffier) to be presented, the position of each carriage with the names of those driven in them, in order of precedence, the exact route, etcetera. Every inch of the way was planned and timed except for the short rest inside my house, where there was to be privacy and relaxation for the royal party.

When we requested that Her Majesty should sign a large photograph of herself to be hung in our Chief Pleas, we were told exactly which photograph we were to buy, and the type of pen that the Queen prefers for signing. This pen is now treasured by the Seneschal, and I have another that she used for signing my book.

As we have only horse-drawn carriages in Sark, one of the difficulties involved in royal visits is the maneuvering to get ahead and receive Royalty when one is part of the carriage procession escorting them. With horses, it is impossible either to soft-pedal or accelerate, so it always means arranging to get to the nearest spot from which one can inconspicuously dash to the doorstep ready to greet the royal personages in a dignified if somewhat breathless manner.

On this occasion, the Seneschal and I had to choose the fastest horse in the island and break away from the procession at the top of the Harbour Hill, from where we drove wildly round by another road in order to arrive at the Chief Pleas before Her Majesty, who had been placed in a carriage drawn by a slower horse. Fortunately, she paused at the War Memorial to inspect our British Legion, which gave us a slight advantage in time.

The ceremony in the Chief Pleas was as follows. As the Queen entered the Chief Pleas the Prévôt announced loudly, *'Sa Majesté La Reine et Son Altesse Royale.'* After calling upon the Greffier to read the opening prayer and the Roll Call, the Queen received a Loyal Address, presented on bended knee by the Seneschal, to which she replied, and then came the moment for me to take the oath of loyalty in the ancient feudal ceremony. We had asked the College of Herald's advice as it could not be traced that this oath had ever before been sworn from a woman to another woman over-lord. The oath in its original form began *'Sire, je suis Votre Homme'* as my father had made it to King George V in Guernsey thirty-four years before. Finally it was arranged that, after approaching Her Majesty and making the traditional three obeisances, I should kneel at her feet holding out my hands palm to palm. The Queen enclosed my hands with her own, and I said in French, *'Ma Souveraine Dame, je Vous rends hommage lige et Vous sera foyale et loyale contre tous.'*

Her Majesty then replied, *'Nous vous acceptons Advouant tous vos légitimes droits et possessions relevant de cette tenure de Nous, sauf pareillement à tous Nos Droits de Régalité.'* I then rose and curtsied, backed to my seat and curtsied again before sitting. The Queen then rose and said, 'Greffier, kindly say the closing prayer,' which is the Gloria in French; then escorted by the Seneschal (Prince Philip accompanied by me) left the building.

It was a memorable and inspiring ceremony, and I felt with a very full heart that it had confirmed the whole meaning of the charter conferred by Her Majesty's predecessor, Queen Elizabeth I in 1565, stressing a sense of continuity as well as providing a lively testimony to the fact that for 392 years Sark has weathered many storms and yet prospered and benefited by the system then granted to it.

After leaving the Chief Pleas the Queen and Prince Philip drove to the field where she was to present the Queen's Cups to the best Guernsey bull and cow on the island. As I am President of the Sark Cattle Society I had to break hastily away again from the procession to get through a gate and rush across the field to meet them on their arrival at the dais which had been erected. After the presentation Her Majesty received a model of a Sark fisherman's boat for the Prince of Wales and a doll dressed in the old Sark costume for Princess Anne.

Following this ceremony, the Queen and Prince Philip walked with me through the garden to my house where Harry and Jehanne were waiting on the doorstep to be presented. During the half-hour's interval, when the party was able to relax quietly in my drawing-room, the Queen told me that she had found the simplicity of the ceremony very interesting and moving. The day's events ended at one o'clock when the Queen boarded the royal barge to embark on the Britannia where she lunched on her way to Alderney.

And now I come to the end of my story.

Our island has progressed and we have moved forward, hoping always to achieve the best and to avoid the pitfalls of new and unwise legislation. Inevitably, there is an opposition to any existing social structure. We have our detractors who seek change and try to discredit our ancient laws and customs, but they would be wise to reflect on the long prosperity of the past, which has depended and still depends on the money brought to Sark by our visitors from overseas, who pay the Landing Tax which provides part of our revenue.

Inherent in most of us is the love of islands. All islands conjure up the stories we have read of pirates, treasure and romance. To one such as myself, who has lived almost entirely on an island, the mainland lacks something indefinable. It may be just the feeling that one cannot encompass it, cannot know all of it. An island is something one can explore until one has an intimate knowledge of every hill and valley, every bay and cove. It is the same delight as a child feels playing at Robinson Crusoe.

Whenever I have travelled in a ship, east or west, I have noticed that people gather on deck to stare, captivated, at any island on the horizon with an interest seldom given to a continent however lovely its outline, and this has encouraged me to write my memories of my own island.

Sark is not only the loveliest and least spoilt of the Channel Islands, it is unparalleled insofar as it has maintained the special privileges granted to it centuries ago. Just so long as my life may be extended, I shall strive to maintain this little feudal paradise with all its traditions, laws and customs, an oasis of quiet and rest, unique in the present-day world.

CPSIA information can be obtained
at www.ICGtesting.com
Printed in the USA
LVHW020739021222
734416LV00002B/363

9 781958 425312